Pocket Rough Guide

Dubai

written and researched by

GAVIN THOMAS

Contents

<< SHEIKH ZAYED ROAD
< BURJ AL ARAB

INTRODUCTION TO
Dubai

Dubai is like nowhere else on the planet. Often claimed to be the world's fastest-growing city, in the past four decades it has metamorphosed from a small Gulf trading centre to become one of the world's most glamorous, spectacular and futuristic urban destinations, fuelled by a heady cocktail of petrodollars, visionary commercial acumen and naked ambition. Dubai's ability to dream – and then achieve – the impossible has ripped up expectations and rewritten the record books, as evidenced by stunning developments such as the soaring Burj Khalifa, the beautiful Burj al Arab and the vast Palm Jumeirah island. Each is a remarkable testament to the ruling sheikhs' determination to make this one of the world's essential destinations for the twenty-first century.

JUMEIRAH MOSQUE

Best places for a Dubai view

Dubai is the world's tallest city and getting your head in the clouds is all part of the experience. The "At the Top" tour to the stunning observation deck of the **Burj Khalifa** (see p.61) is unmissable, while the best bars for a bird's-eye view include **Neos** (see p.67), **Bar 44** (see p.87) and **Up on the Tenth** (see p.49).

Modern Dubai is often seen as a panegyric to consumerist luxury: a self-indulgent haven of magical hotels, superlative restaurants and extravagantly themed shopping malls. Perhaps not surprisingly the city is often stereotyped as a vacuous consumerist fleshpot, appealing only to those with more cash than culture, although this one-eyed cliché does absolutely no justice to Dubai's beguiling contrasts and rich cultural make-up. The city's headline-grabbing mega-projects have also deflected attention from Dubai's massive but largely unappreciated role in providing the Islamic world with a model of political stability, religious tolerance and business acumen in action. In one of the world's most troubled regions this peaceful and progressive pan-Arabian global city serves as the ultimate symbol of what can be achieved. Dubai also ranks among the world's most multicultural cities, featuring a cosmopolitan cast of Emiratis, Arabs, Iranians, Indians, Filipinos and Europeans – a fascinating patchwork of peoples and languages which gives the city its uniquely varied cultural appeal.

For the visitor, there's far more to Dubai than designer boutiques and five-star hotels – although of course if all you're looking for is a luxurious dose of sun, sand and shopping, the city takes some beating. If you want to step beyond the tourist clichés, however, you'll find that Dubai has much more to offer than you might think. The old city centre serves up many fascinating reminders of Dubai's past, including the grand old wind-towered mansions of Bastakiya and Shindagha; the stately wooden dhows, which still moor up alongside the breezy Creek; and, of course, the helter-skelter souks of Bur Dubai and Deira, piled high with traditional Arabian jewellery, scents and spices – frankincense from Somalia, bedouin necklaces from Oman, rose leaves from Iran, and much more. The city's modern attractions are equally memorable, ranging from world-famous

SPICE SOUK

contemporary icons like the futuristic Burj Khalifa, the world's tallest building – and the iconic, sail-shaped Burj al Arab through to myriad quirkier attractions – kitsch faux-Arabian bazaars, ersatz pyramids, zany themed shopping malls and a string of other wonderful, wacky and sometimes downright weird modern developments. In addition, Dubai is within easy striking distance of a number of other rewarding day-trip destinations, including Sharjah, home to some fine museums, the laidback inland oasis city of Al Ain and the vibrant megalopolis of Abu Dhabi, capital of the UAE.

The recent credit crunch hit Dubai hard, pushing the city to the verge of bankruptcy and signalling the end of some of the more extravagant mega-projects (including, for example, an artificial archipelago in the shape of the solar system and the world's biggest theme park, complete with animatronic dinosaurs and a life-sized replica of the Taj Mahal, to mention just two). Pronouncements of the city's demise are likely to prove premature, however, and Dubai remains one of the twenty-first century's most fascinating and vibrant urban experiments in progress. Visit now to see history, literally, in the making.

When to visit

The best time to visit Dubai is in the cooler winter months from December through to February, with average daily temperatures in the mid-20s °C. Temperatures rise significantly from March through to April, and in October and November, when the thermometer regularly nudges up into the 30s. From May to September the city boils – July and August are especially suffocating – with average temperatures in the high 30s to low 40s (and frequently higher). Room rates at most of the top hotels fall during this period, sometimes dramatically, making the summer an excellent time to enjoy some authentic Dubaian luxury at relatively affordable prices. Rainfall is rare for most of the year, although there are usually a few wet days during January and February.

DUBAI AT A GLANCE

>> EATING

It's almost impossible not to eat well in Dubai, whatever your budget. There's inexpensive food galore in the curry houses of **Bur Dubai** and **Karama** and at the shwarma stands and Lebanese-style cafés of **Deira**, **Satwa** and elsewhere, while both home-grown and international cafés and fast-food chains citywide provide further affordable options. Virtually all the city's more upscale restaurants are located in hotels – many of the best can be found in **Sheikh Zayed Road/Downtown Dubai**, or along the coast in the **Dubai Marina** or around the **Burj al Arab**.

>> DRINKING

You won't go thirsty in Dubai, although alcohol is generally only served in hotel bars, pubs and restaurants. Many hotel bars tend to (vaguely) resemble British-style **pubs**, with pints and inexpensive counter food served, though **cocktail bars** are the norm in more upmarket places, including a number of spectacular high-rise venues in flashy skyscrapers, and more chilled-out, Arabian-style places, especially around the **Burj al Arab**, **Dubai Marina** beach and the **Palm Jumeirah**. Alcohol doesn't come cheap, although most pubs run some kind of **happy hour**. In addition, many places also host regular **ladies' nights** (usually Tuesday or Wednesday) offering women complimentary tipples.

>> SHOPPING

Shopping in Dubai takes two forms. First, there are the old-fashioned souks of **Bur Dubai**, **Karama** and, especially, **Deira**, good for traditional items like gold, perfume and spices (not to mention a roaring trade in designer fakes), and with bargaining the norm. Then there's the city's spectacular collection of supersized malls, packed to the gills with every consumer desirable imaginable. Head to the gargantuan **Dubai Mall** for the ultimate retail experience, while the sprawling **Mall of the Emirates** is another must-shop. More manageable retail destinations include the **BurJuman**, **Mercato** and **Marina** malls and the enjoyable **Wafi/Khan Murjan** complex.

>> NIGHTLIFE

Nightlife in Dubai takes various forms. Locals tend to hit the city's myriad **malls**, which stay open till late and remain remarkably busy right up until midnight. Visitors usually head for the city's **restaurants** and **bars** – many of the latter host regular live music or DJs – while it's also fun to hang out in a **shisha café**, puffing on a waterpipe. There's also a growing number of **clubs**, and although many places are mainly about pouting and posing, there are some good, unpretentious venues. Cultural attractions are usually a bit thin on the ground, although things improve significantly during the Dubai jazz and film **festivals**.

OUR RECOMMENDATIONS FOR WHERE TO EAT, DRINK AND SHOP ARE LISTED AT THE END OF EACH PLACES CHAPTER.

Day One in Dubai

1 Deira Gold Souk > p.42. Browse the shop windows of Deira's most famous souk, stuffed with vast quantities of gold and precious stones.

2 Heritage House and Al Ahmadiya School > p.43. Catch a rare glimpse of life in old Dubai at this pair of neatly restored traditional houses.

3 Dhow Wharfage > p.45. A little slice of living maritime history, with dozens of antique wooden dhows moored up alongside the Creek.

4 Cross the Creek by abra > p.37. Jump on board one of these old-fashioned wooden ferries for the memorable short crossing to Bur Dubai.

Lunch > p.40. Relax over a light lunch in the beautiful garden of the *Arabian Tea House Café*.

5 Bastakiya > p.35. Get lost amid the winding alleyways and wind-towered houses of Dubai's most perfectly preserved old quarter.

6 Dubai Museum > p.33. Explore the emirate's history at this enjoyable museum, housed in quaint Al Fahidi Fort – the city's oldest building.

7 A walk along the Creek > p.32. Walk past the Grand Mosque and through the Textile Souk and out along the breezy creekside to Shindagha.

8 Sheikh Saeed al Maktoum House > p.38. A fascinating collection of historical photographs showcases the rapidly changing face of Dubai.

Dinner > p.40. Settle down for a supper of excellent, inexpensive mezze and grills at *Kan Zaman*.

Day Two in Dubai

1 Walk down Sheikh Zayed Road
> p.58. Start at the stunning Emirates Towers and wander south along Sheikh Zayed Road, Dubai's most flamboyantly futuristic architectural parade.

2 Dubai Mall > p.61. Dive into the city's mall to end all malls, offering endless hours of retail therapy and a host of other entertainments.

3 At the Top, Burj Khalifa > p.61. Ride the world's fastest elevators to the spectacular observation deck on the 124th floor of the world's tallest building.

Lunch > p.63. Grab an outside table at the very civilized *More* café, with sweeping views of the Dubai Fountain and Burj Khalifa.

4 Wild Wadi > p.74. Swim, splash and slide your way around the pools, rivers and rapids of the entertaining Wild Wadi water park.

Afternoon tea, Burj al Arab > p.72 & p.79. Indulge in an opulent afternoon tea in the iconic, "seven-star" Burj al Arab's *Skyview Bar* or *Sahn Eddar Lounge*.

5 Souk Madinat Jumeirah > p.75. Walk over to the stunning Madinat Jumeirah complex, with its picture-perfect waterways and old-fashioned souk.

Dinner > p.78 & p.79. Eat a memorable meal above the water at *Pierchic*, with fabulous views of the Burj, Madinat Jumeirah and coast. Then head on to the gorgeous *Bahri Bar* for a drink or two, perhaps rounded off with a visit to the city's new superclub, *Pacha*.

Souks and shopping

For a taste of retail therapy, Dubai style, you'll need to explore both the city's traditional souks and its shiny modern malls.

1 Gold Souk > p.42. Haggle for bangles, bracelets and necklaces at Deira's bustling Gold Souk.

2 Perfume Souk > p.45. Check out the local and international scents – or make up your own bespoke fragrance.

3 Covered Souk > p.46. Wander through the covered market's endless maze of alleyways – getting lost is half the fun.

4 Wafi > p.51. One of the city's smoothest shopping experiences with one of its coolest collections of independent fashion labels.

5 Khan Murjan Souk > p.51. Explore the myriad shops of the pretty Khan Murjan, bursting with Arabian scents, jewellery, textiles, furniture and much more.

Lunch > p.56. The enjoyable *Khan Murjan Restaurant* serves up Middle Eastern cuisine in a good-looking outdoor courtyard.

6 Ibn Battuta Mall > p.84. Catch the metro down to Dubai's most eye-catching mall, extravagantly themed after Ibn Battuta's travels.

7 Mall of the Emirates > p.75. Perhaps the city's most satisfying all-in-one retail destination, with 500-odd shops to explore.

Dinner > p.77. Have dinner at *Après*, with tasty international cuisine, crisp cocktails and fine views over surreal Ski Dubai next door.

Hidden Dubai

To escape the crowds, head for some of Dubai's less well-known attractions – although you'll need a car or taxi for the latter part of the day.

1 Naif Museum > p.46. This little-visited museum showcases the engaging history of the Dubai police force since colonial times.

2 Al Wasl and Covered souks > p.46. Walk down Al Musallah Street then dive west into the tangle of little streets and alleyways of the disorienting Al Wasl Souk.

3 Hindi Lane > p.36. Take an abra across the Creek to Bur Dubai's Textile Souk, just a few steps from this entertaining little Indian enclave of Hindi Lane.

Lunch > p.40. The lovely little *XVA Café* is close to Hindi Lane, tucked away at the back of Bastakiya.

4 Iranian mosques > p.36. It's a short walk through the Textile Souk to Bur Dubai's fine pair of Iranian Shia'a mosques.

5 Ras al Khor Wildlife Sanctuary > p.54. Take a taxi out to the Ras al Khor Wildlife Sanctuary, with flocks of vivid pink flamingoes incongruously framed against distant skyscrapers.

6 Majlis Ghorfat um al Sheif > p.70. This picturesque old mud-brick house is incongruously marooned amid the villas of Jumeirah.

Dinner > p.56. Grab a pavement table at the always bustling *Al Mallah* Lebanese café in the personable suburb of Satwa, a part of the city usually overlooked by tourists.

Big sights

1 Burj Khalifa The world's tallest building, rising like an enormous space rocket above Downtown Dubai. > **p.61**

3 Deira souks An intricate tangle of bazaars piled high with gold, spices, perfumes and more. > **pp.42–46**

2 Bastakiya Fascinating little labyrinth of old-fashioned houses topped by innumerable wind towers. > **p.35**

4 The Creek The original heart of old Dubai, best appreciated from aboard an old-fashioned abra. > **p.32 & p.37**

5 Burj al Arab Superb, sail-shaped hotel towering above the coast of southern Dubai. > **p.72 & p.108**

Shopping

1 Ibn Battuta Mall Mile-long mall themed after the journeys of Moroccan traveller Ibn Battuta. > **p.84**

2 Dubai Mall The world's biggest mall, with over 1200 shops cheek by jowl. > **p.61**

4 Khan Murjan Souk Sumptuous ersatz Arabian bazaar, with the city's best selection of craft shops. > **p.51**

3 Mall of the Emirates Huge array of classy boutiques next to the surreal Ski Dubai snowdrome. > **p.75**

5 Souk Madinat Jumeirah Superb souk in traditional style at the heart of Madinat Jumeirah complex. > **p.75**

Restaurants

1 Pierchic Upmarket seafood in a superb ocean setting with magnificent views of the Burj al Arab. **> p.78**

2 Buddha Bar Bags of Oriental cool, excellent pan-Asian food and crisp cocktails. **> p.85**

3 La Petite Maison Memorable blend of old-school French elegance and sunny *niçoise*-style cooking. **> p.64**

4 Table 9 by Nick and Scott Top-class yet affordable contemporary dining in an informal setting. **> p.49**

5 Indego by Vineet Innovative modern subcontinental cooking by culinary maestro Vineet Bhatia. **> p.86**

Traditional Dubai

1 Jumeirah Mosque Dubai's most beautiful mosque – open to visitors during informative guided tours. ➤ **p.68**

2 Dhow Wharfage Dozens of superb Arabian dhows moored up along the Deira creekside. > **p.45**

4 Dubai Museum Comprehensive and enjoyable introduction to the city's history and traditional culture. > **p.33**

3 Sheikh Saeed al Maktoum House Former home of the ruling sheikhs, now an absorbing museum. > **p.38**

5 Gold Souk One of the cheapest places in the world to stock up on gold jewellery. > **p.42**

Hotels

1 **Jumeirah Zabeel Saray** Marvellously opulent and seriously over-the-top Ottoman-themed palace on the Palm. **>** **p.109**

2 Grosvenor House Cooler than a polar bear on ice, with suave decor and superb restaurants, bars and spas. > **p.109**

3 One&Only Royal Mirage
Dubai's most romantic hotel, with gorgeous Moorish decor and palm trees galore. > **p.110**

4 Park Hyatt Serene Moroccan-style hotel in a picture-perfect creekside setting. > **p.106**

5 Bab al Shams Desert Resort and Spa Stylish retreat offering an authentic taste of life among the sands. > **p.110**

Kids' Dubai

1 Dubai Aquarium Walk through an underwater glass tunnel and learn about unusual marine creatures. > **p.61**

2 Wild Wadi Wildly popular water park with a huge variety of slides, rides and pools. > **p.74**

4 Ferrari World Rides, roller coasters and plenty of adrenaline at the world's largest indoor theme park. > **p.123**

3 Dubai Dolphinarium Swim with dolphins or just take in one of the cheesy but enjoyable shows. > **p.123**

5 Children's City Fun edutainment in a wacky Lego-like creekside complex. > **p.123**

Bars

1 Bahri Bar Gorgeous Moroccan styling – and even more gorgeous views over the Burj al Arab. > **p.79**

2 101 Dining Lounge and Bar Sweeping views of coast and Marina from this chic waterfront terrace bar. > **p.86**

3 360° Seductive chill-out venue at the end of a breakwater overlooking the *Jumeirah Beach Hotel.* > **p.78**

4 Bar 44 Smooth cocktail bar with unmatched views over the massed Marina skyscrapers. > **p.87**

5 Rooftop Bar One of Dubai's most romantic bars, with superb Arabian-themed decor. > **p.87**

Out of the city

1 **Desert safaris** Go dune-bashing or try your hand at sand-skiing. > **p.118**

3 Sheikh Zayed Mosque, Abu Dhabi Magnificent modern mosque, with a spectacularly opulent prayer hall within. > **p.100**

2 Emirates Palace Hotel, Abu Dhabi Vast Arabian-themed city landmark, and one of the region's most extravagant places to stay. > **p.96 & p.111**

4 Sharjah Museum of Islamic Civilization State-of-the-art museum showcasing the history, arts and scientific contributions of the Islamic world. > **p.88**

5 Al Ain Oasis Shady plantations of luxuriant date palms in the heart of Al Ain. > **p.92**

PLACES

Bur Dubai

Strung out along the southern side of the Creek, Bur Dubai is the oldest part of the city. Parts of the district's historic waterfront still retain their engagingly old-fashioned appearance, with a quaint tangle of sand-coloured buildings and a distinctively Arabian skyline, spiked with dozens of wind towers and the occasional minaret. At the heart of the district, the absorbing Dubai Museum offers an excellent introduction to the city's history, while the old Iranian quarter of Bastakiya is home to the city's most impressive collection of traditional buildings. Heading west along the Creek, the old-fashioned Textile Souk is the prettiest in the city, while to the north the historic quarter of Shindagha is home to another fine cluster of century-old edifices.

THE CREEK

MAP P.34, POCKET MAP M11–N10

Cutting a broad, salty swathe through the middle of the city centre, **the Creek** (Al Khor in Arabic) lies physically and historically at the very heart of Dubai. The Creek was the location of the earliest

settlements in the area – first on the Bur Dubai side of the water, and subsequently in Deira – and also played a crucial role in establishing Dubai as a major port during the twentieth century. Commerce aside, the Creek remains the centrepiece of Dubai and its finest natural feature; a broad, serene stretch of water which is as essential a part of the fabric and texture of the city as the Thames is to London or the Seine to Paris.

The walk along the Bur Dubai waterfront is particularly lovely, pedestrianized throughout, and with cooling breezes and wonderful views of the city down the Creek – particularly beautiful towards sunset. For the best views, begin in Shindagha (see p.37) and head south; it takes about 20–25 minutes to reach Bastakiya. A spacious promenade stretches down the waterfront as far as Shindagha Tower, from where a narrow walkway extends down to the Bur Dubai Abra Station and the Textile Souk.

DUBAI MUSEUM

Al Fahidi St. Al Fahidi metro ☎ 04 353 1862,
ⓦ bit.ly/DubaiMuseum. Sat–Thurs
8.30am–8.30pm, Fri 7.30–8.30pm. 3dh.
MAP P.34, POCKET MAP M12

DUBAI MUSEUM

At the dead centre of Bur Dubai stands the old **Al Fahidi Fort**, a rough-and-ready little structure whose engagingly lopsided corner turrets – one square and one round – make it look a bit like a giant sandcastle. Dating from around 1800, the fort is the oldest building in Dubai, having originally been built to defend the town's landward approaches against raids by rival Bedouin tribes; it also served as the residence and office of the ruling sheikh up until the early twentieth century before being converted into a museum in 1971.

The fort now provides a home for the excellent **Dubai Museum**, a logical first stop on any tour of the city and the perfect place to get up to speed with the history and culture of the emirate. Entering the museum you step into the fort's central **courtyard**, dotted with assorted wooden boats revealing the different types of vessel used in old Dubai, including a traditional abra, not so very different from those still in service on the Creek today (see box, p.37). In one corner stands a traditional *barasti* (or *areesh*) hut, topped by a basic burlap wind tower – the sort of building most people in Dubai lived in right up until the 1960s. The hut's walls are made out of neatly cut palm branches, spaced so that breezes are able to blow right through and meaning it stays surprisingly cool even in the heat of the day.

The museum's real attraction, however, is its sprawling **underground section**, a buried wonderland which offers as comprehensive an overview of the traditional life, crafts and culture of Dubai as you'll find anywhere. A sequence of rooms – full of the sound effects and life-size mannequins without which no Dubai museum would be complete – covers every significant aspect of traditional Dubaian life, including Islam, local architecture and wind towers, traditional dress and games, camels and falconry. Interesting short films on various subjects are shown in many of the rooms, including fascinating historic footage of pearl divers at work. There's also a line of shops featuring various traditional trades and crafts – carpenters, blacksmiths, tailors, spice merchants and so on. It's kitsch but undeniably engaging, populated with colourful mannequins in traditional dress, although the old black-and-white video clips of artisans at work add a slightly spooky touch.

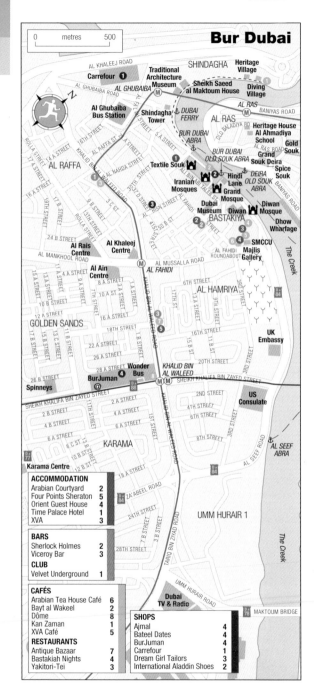

Bur Dubai

0 metres 500

ACCOMMODATION
Arabian Courtyard	2
Four Points Sheraton	5
Orient Guest House	4
Time Palace Hotel	1
XVA	3

BARS
Sherlock Holmes	2
Viceroy Bar	3

CLUB
Velvet Underground	1

CAFÉS
Arabian Tea House Café	6
Bayt al Wakeel	2
Dôme	8
Kan Zaman	1
XVA Café	5

RESTAURANTS
Antique Bazaar	7
Bastakiah Nights	4
Yakitori-Tei	3

SHOPS
Ajmal	4
Bateel Dates	4
BurJuman	4
Carrefour	1
Dream Girl Tailors	3
International Aladdin Shoes	2

BASTAKIYA

Al Fahidi metro. Coins Museum ☎ 04 353
9090; Sat–Thurs 8am–8pm. Architectural
Heritage Department Sun–Thurs 8am–2pm.
Majlis Gallery ☎ 04 353 6233,
ⓦ themajlisgallery.com; Sat–Thurs
10am–6pm. MAP P.34, POCKET MAP N12

The beautiful old quarter of
Bastakiya comprises a
photogenic huddle of traditional
Gulf houses, capped with
dozens of wind towers and
arranged around a rabbit warren
of tiny alleyways. The houses
here were originally put up in
the early 1900s by merchants
from southern Iran who named
their new suburb Bastakiya after
their ancestral home, the
Iranian town of Bastak.

A number of old Bastakiya
houses have now been opened
to the public as small-scale
museums and galleries. Best is
the **Coins Museum**, containing
a well-presented collection of
over four hundred Islamic
coins. The **Architectural
Heritage Department**, boasting
a particularly large and chintzy
courtyard and fine views over
Bastakiya from its roof, also
repays a quick look. Also worth
a visit is the long-running
Majlis Gallery, the oldest in the
city, founded in 1989 and
hosting monthly exhibitions
showcasing the work of Emirati
and international artists.

WIND TOWERS, BASTAKIYA

THE SMCCU

Near Al Fahidi Roundabout. Al Fahidi metro
☎ 04 353 6666, ⓦ cultures.ae. Sun–Thurs
8am–6pm, Sat 9am–1pm. MAP P.34,
POCKET MAP N12

Based in an office on the eastern
edge of Bastakiya, the
pioneering **Sheikh Mohammed
Centre for Cultural Understanding**, or **SMCCU**, runs
popular tours of Jumeirah
Mosque (see p.68) and a
number of activities in
Bastakiya itself, including
walking tours, Gulf Arabic
classes and "cultural" breakfasts
and lunches, during which you
get the chance to sample some
traditional food while chatting
to the centre's Emirati staff.

Wind towers

Often described as the world's oldest form of air-conditioning, the
distinctive **wind towers** (*barjeel*) that top many old Dubai buildings
(as well as numerous modern ones constructed in faux-Arabian style)
provided an ingeniously simple way of countering the Gulf's searing
temperatures in a pre-electrical age. Rising around 6m above the rooftops
on which they're built, wind towers are open on all four sides and channel
any available breezes down into the building via triangular flues. Bastakiya's
collection of wind towers is the largest and finest in the city, with subtle
variations in design from tower to tower, meaning that no two are ever
exactly alike.

THE GRAND MOSQUE AND DIWAN

Next to the Al Fahidi Fort, Ali bin Abi Taleb St. Al Fahidi metro. No entry to non-Muslims. MAP P.34, POCKET MAP M11 & N12

The biggest in Dubai, the imposing **Grand Mosque** is an impressively large if rather plain structure, the general austerity relieved only by an elaborate swirl of Koranic script over the entrance and the city's tallest minaret. Hugging the creekside immediately east of the Grand Mosque sits the **Diwan**, or Ruler's Court, now home to assorted government functionaries, and the eye-catching **Diwan Mosque**, topped by an unusually flattened onion dome and a slender white minaret which rivals that of the nearby Grand Mosque in height.

THE TEXTILE SOUK

Al Ghubaiba metro. MAP P.34, POCKET MAP M11

At the heart of Bur Dubai, the **Textile Souk** (also sometimes referred to as the "Old Souk") is easily the prettiest in the city, occupying an immaculately restored traditional bazaar, its long line of sand-coloured buildings shaded by a fine arched wooden roof, blissfully

TEXTILE SOUK

cool even in the heat of the day and illuminated by traditional Moorish hanging lights after dark. This was once the most important bazaar in the city although its commercial importance has long since faded and almost all the shops have now been taken over by Indian traders flogging reams of sari cloth and fluorescent blankets, alongside assorted tourist tat (if you're hankering for an I ♥ DUBAI T-shirt or spangly camel, now's your chance).

HINDI LANE

Textile Souk. Al Fahidi metro. MAP P.34, POCKET MAP M11

The colourful little alleyway popularly known as **Hindi Lane** is one of Dubai's most curious and appealing little ethnic enclaves. Walk to the far (eastern) end of the Textile Souk, turn right by T. Singh Trading and then left by Mohammadi Textiles and you'll find yourself in a tiny alleyway lined with picturesque little Indian shops selling an array of bangles, bindis, coconuts, flowers, bells, almanacs and other religious paraphernalia. On the north side of Hindi Lane is the tiny hybridized Hindu-cum-Sikh temple sometimes referred to as the **Sikh Gurudaba**, while continuing along Hindi Lane to the back of the Grand Mosque brings you to a second Hindu temple, the **Shri Nathje Jayate Temple**, dedicated to Krishna.

IRANIAN MOSQUES

Ali bin Abi Taleb St (11c St). Al Ghubaiba metro. No entry to non-Muslims. MAP P.34, POCKET MAP M11

Hidden away on the south side of the Textile Souk are two of the city's finest **Iranian mosques**. The more easterly of the two mosques is particularly

Crossing the Creek by abra

One of the most fun things you can do in Bur Dubai is go for a ride by abra (see p.116) across the Creek – the area's two main abra stations are the **Bur Dubai Abra Station**, just outside the main entrance to the Textile Souk, and **Bur Dubai Old Souk Abra Station**, inside the souk itself, from where these old-fashioned little wooden boats shuttle across the Creek at all hours of the day and night to **Deira Old Souk** and **Al Sabkha** abra stations on the other side of the water in Deira. The boats' basic design has changed little for at least a century, apart from the addition of a diesel engine, and abras still play a crucial role in the city's transport infrastructure, carrying a staggering twenty million passengers per year for a modest 1dh per trip.

eye-catching, with a superb facade and dome covered in a lustrous mosaic of predominantly blue tiling decorated with geometrical floral motifs. The second mosque, about 50m west along the road, close to the *Time Palace Hotel*, is a contrastingly plain, sand-coloured building, its rooftop enlivened by four tightly packed little egg-shaped domes.

AL FAHIDI STREET

Al Fahidi and Khalid bin al Waleed metros.
MAP P.34, POCKET MAP M11–N12

Al Fahidi Street is Bur Dubai's de facto high street, lined with a mix of shops selling Indian

IRANIAN MOSQUE

clothing, shoes and jewellery along with other places stacked high with mobile phones and fancy watches (not necessarily genuine). The eastern end of the street and adjacent Al Hisn Street are also often loosely referred to as **Meena Bazaar**, the centre of the district's textile and tailoring industry and home to a dense razzle-dazzle of shopfronts stuffed with sumptuous saris.

SHINDAGHA

MAP P.34, POCKET MAP M10–N10

Although now effectively swallowed up by Bur Dubai, the historic creekside district of **Shindagha** was, until fifty years ago, a quite separate and self-contained area occupying its own spit of land, and frequently cut off from Bur Dubai proper during high tides. This was once the most exclusive address in town, home to the ruling family and other local elites, who occupied a series of imposing houses lined up along the waterfront. The edge of the district is guarded by the distinctive waterfront **Shindagha Tower**, instantly recognizable thanks to the slit windows and protruding buttress on each side, arranged to resemble a human face.

SHEIKH SAEED AL MAKTOUM HOUSE

Architecture Museum, halfway between Shindagha Tower and Sheikh Saeed al Maktoum House, occupies a rather grand traditional house with the usual sandy courtyard, wind towers and elaborate latticed wall-panels decorated with geometrical and floral patterns moulded from the traditional mix of gypsum, coral, limestone and sand. Inside, informative displays cover the story of architecture in the Emirates generally and Dubai in particular, including insightful explanations of the region's various different types of building, local materials and construction techniques, accompanied by a good spread of exhibits and the usual life-size mannequins pounding and plastering silently away.

SHEIKH SAEED AL MAKTOUM HOUSE

Shindagha waterfront. Al Ghubaiba metro
☎ 04 393 7139, ✪ bit.ly/SheikhSaeedHouse.
Sat–Thurs 8am–8.30pm, Fri 3–9.30pm. 2dh.
MAP P.34, POCKET MAP M10

Standing on the beautiful Shindagha waterfront, the **Sheikh Saeed al Maktoum House** is one of Dubai's most interesting museums, occupying what from 1896 to 1958 was the principal residence of Dubai's ruling family – an atmospheric wind-towered mansion arranged around a spacious sandy courtyard. Inside, pride of place goes to the superb collection of old **photographs**, with images of the city from the 1940s through to the late 1960s, showing the first steps in its amazing transformation from a remote Gulf town to global megalopolis.

TRADITIONAL ARCHITECTURE MUSEUM

Shindagha waterfront. Al Ghubaiba metro
☎ 04 392 0093, ✪ bit.ly/ArchMusDubai.
Sat–Thurs 7am–6pm, Fri 8am–6pm. Free.
MAP P.34, POCKET MAP M10

One of the most interesting of the hotchpotch of Shindagha museums, the **Traditional**

HERITAGE AND DIVING VILLAGES

Shindagha waterfront. Al Ghubaiba metro
☎ 04 393 7139, ✪ bit.ly/HeritageDiving.
Sun–Thurs 8.30am–10.30pm, Fri & Sat 4.30–10.30pm. Free. MAP P.34, POCKET MAP N18

The so-called **Heritage Village** comprises a string of traditional buildings surrounding a large sandy courtyard, at the back of which are a few souvenir shops. The atmosphere is fairly moribund at most times, but livens up somewhat after dark during national holidays and festivals, particularly Ramadan and the Dubai Shopping Festival, when locals put on cookery and craft displays. The adjacent **Diving Village** offers more of the same, with further traditional buildings around another courtyard dotted with a couple of wooden boats and a few *barasti* huts, plus two boat-shaped phone booths – a rather lame tribute to the pearl-diving trade which underpinned the city's economy up until the 1930s.

Shops

AJMAL

BurJuman. Khalid bin al Waleed metro
☎ 04 351 5505, ⓦ ajmalperfume.com. Daily
10am–10pm (Thurs & Fri until 11pm). MAP P.34,
POCKET MAP M3

Dubai's leading perfumiers,
offering a wide range of
fragrances including traditional
attar-based Arabian scents. If
you don't like any of their
ready-made perfumes you can
make up your own from the big
glass bottles on display behind
the counter. Other branches at
Deira Gold Souk, Khan Murjan,
Deira City Centre and Mall of
the Emirates.

BATEEL DATES

BurJuman. Khalid bin al Waleed metro ☎ 04
355 2853, ⓦ bateel.com. Daily 10am–10pm
(Thurs & Fri until 11pm). MAP P.34, POCKET MAP M3

The best dates in the city, grown
in Bateel's own plantations in
Saudi Arabia and sold either
plain, covered in chocolate or
stuffed with ingredients such as
almonds and slices of lemon or
orange. Other branches at Deira
City Centre, Festival Centre,
Souk al Bahar and Dubai Mall.

BURJUMAN

Corner of Khalid bin al Waleed and Sheikh
Zayed roads. Khalid bin al Waleed metro
(exit 3) ☎ 04 352 0222, ⓦ burjuman.com.
Daily 10am–10pm (Thurs & Fri until 11pm).
MAP P.34, POCKET MAP M3

The biggest and best city-centre
mall, BurJuman remains
popular thanks to its convenient
location and 300-plus shops,
including the flagship Saks Fifth
Avenue department store.

CARREFOUR

Al Ghubaiba Rd. Al Ghubaiba metro
☎ 04 393 5601, ⓦ carrefouruae.com.
Daily 9am–midnight. MAP P.34, POCKET MAP L10

This vast French hypermarket
chain might not be the most
atmospheric place to shop in
the city, but it is one of the best
places to pick up just about
any kind of Middle Eastern
foodstuff you fancy, and is
also a good source of cheap
electronics, kitchenware, rugs
and perfumes. Other branches
at Deira City Centre, Mall of
the Emirates and Marina Mall.

DREAM GIRL TAILORS

Al Hisn St. Al Fahidi metro ☎ 04 388 0070.
Daily 10am–1pm & 4–10pm, Fri 6–9pm only.
MAP P.34, POCKET MAP L12

Perhaps the best of the various
tailors hereabouts, offering
well-made, inexpensive copies
of any existing garment you
might bring in: around 60dh for
a shirt or trousers, or from
150dh for a dress (not including
material). They can also make
up clothes from photographs or
even a hand-drawn design.

INTERNATIONAL ALADDIN SHOES

Textile Souk (next to Bur Dubai Old Souk Abra
Station). Al Ghubaiba metro ☎ 055 515 4351.
Daily 8am–11pm. MAP P.34, POCKET MAP M11

Eye-catching little stall (no sign)
in the midst of the Textile Souk
selling a gorgeous selection of
colourful embroidered ladies'
slippers (65–200dh) along with
lovely embroidered belts.

ARABIAN TEA HOUSE CAFÉ

Cafés

ARABIAN TEA HOUSE CAFÉ

Al Fahidi St, next to the main entrance to
Bastakiya. Al Fahidi metro ☎ 04 353 5071,
ⓦfacebook.com/ArabianTeaHouseCafe. Daily
8am–8pm. MAP P.34, POCKET MAP N12
Lovely little courtyard café set
in the idyllic garden of a
traditional old Bastakiya house.
The menu features a good
range of light meals, plus
sandwiches and salads (from
30dh), assorted breakfasts
(from 22dh) and decent juices
and smoothies.

BAYT AL WAKEEL

Mackenzie House, near the main entrance
of the Textile Souk. Al Ghubaiba metro
☎ 04 353 0530. Daily noon–midnight.
MAP P.34, POCKET MAP M11
The small menu of rather
pedestrian Arabian food (plus a
few Chinese options) won't win
any awards, but the convenient
location near the entrance to
the Textile Souk and the setting
on an attractive terrace jutting
out into the Creek amply
compensate. Mezze 15dh,
mains 30–40dh (plus some
more expensive seafood dishes
60–75dh).

DÔME

BurJuman. Khalid bin al Waleed metro
☎ 04 355 6004, ⓦdomecafes.ae. Daily
8am–10pm. MAP P.34, POCKET MAP M3
This low-key café is a reliable
source of good coffee and
cheap grub including pasta,
pizzas, soups, salads, burgers
and a few more substantial
international mains, plus very
competitively priced daily
specials, with mains for around
27–42dh. Other branches at
DIFC, Dubai Mall, Jumaira
Plaza, Souk Madinat Jumeirah
and Ibn Battuta Mall.

KAN ZAMAN

Next to the Diving Village. Shindagha. Al
Ghubaiba metro ☎ 04 393 9913, ⓦalkoufa
.com. Daily 11am–3.30am. MAP P.34.
POCKET MAP N10
Occupying a beautiful
creekside location in historic
Shindagha, this large Middle
Eastern restaurant is one of
the best places in the city for
a blast of authentic Arabian
atmosphere – it's usually full of
local Emiratis and expat Arabs
puffing on shisha after dark.
Food includes good hot and
cold mezze (most under 20dh)
plus meat and seafood grills
(40dh), and there's an excellent
shisha collection.

XVA CAFÉ

Bastakiya. Al Fahidi metro ☎ 04 353 5383,
ⓦxvahotel.com. Daily except Fri 9am–7pm.
MAP P.34, POCKET MAP N12
Tucked away in an alley at the
back of Bastakiya, this shady
courtyard café (attached to a
lovely guesthouse; see p.105)
serves up good vegetarian food
including flavoursome salads
and sandwiches (22–33dh) and
assorted light meals (33–38dh)
with a Middle Eastern twist –
tabbouleh or burghul salads,
for example, or halloumi and
cucumber sandwiches – plus
good breakfasts.

Restaurants

ANTIQUE BAZAAR

Four Points Sheraton, Khalid bin al Waleed Rd. Al Fahidi metro ☎ 04 397 7333, ⓦ antiquebazaar-dubai.com. Daily 12.30–3pm & 7.30pm–2.30am, closed Fri lunch. MAP P.34, POCKET MAP M13

This pretty little restaurant, littered with assorted subcontinental artefacts, dishes up a fair selection of North Indian favourites with reasonable aplomb. There's also a decent resident band and dancers nightly from 9pm. Mains from around 40dh (veg), 50–55dh (meat).

BASTAKIAH NIGHTS

Bastakiya. Al Fahidi metro ☎ 04 353 7772, ⓦ facebook.com (search for "Bastakiah N Rest"). Daily 11am–11pm. MAP P.34, POCKET MAP N12

One of the most beautiful places to eat in central Dubai, occupying a superbly restored old house in Bastakiya. The Middle Eastern food (mains 45–70dh) doesn't quite match up, though when the setting's this good you might not care.

YAKITORI-TEI

Ascot Hotel, Khalid bin al Waleed Rd. Al Fahidi metro ☎ 04 352 0900, ⓦ facebook.com /YakitoriTeiAscotHotel. Daily 12.30–3pm (last orders) & 6.30–11.30pm. MAP P.34, POCKET MAP L11

Though this modern establishment lacks a bit of character, its mainly Japanese menu (mains mostly 55–85dh) ticks all the usual boxes, with decent stir-fries, sushi, sashimi, maki, yakitori and curries. There's also a cursory list of Thai classics and jugs of draught sake to wash it all down with.

Bars

SHERLOCK HOLMES

Arabian Courtyard Hotel, Al Fahidi St. Al Fahidi metro ☎ 04 351 9111. Daily noon–2am (no alcohol served 4–6pm). MAP P.34, POCKET MAP M12

One of the better pubs hereabouts, with a relaxed atmosphere, flock wallpaper and glass cases full of vaguely Sherlock Holmes-related memorabilia – although noisy live music sometimes intrudes. Also does decent pub food.

VICEROY BAR

Four Points Sheraton Hotel, Khalid bin al Waleed Rd. Al Fahidi metro ☎ 04 397 7444. Daily 12.30pm–midnight. MAP P.34, POCKET MAP M13

This traditional English-style pub is the nicest in Bur Dubai, complete with fake oak-beamed ceiling, authentic wooden bar and oodles of comfy leather armchairs.

Club

VELVET UNDERGROUND

Royal Ascot Hotel, Khalid bin al Waleed Rd. Al Fahidi metro ☎ 050 962 4222, ⓦ velvetundergrounddubai.com. Tues–Sun 10.30pm–3am. MAP P.34, POCKET MAP L11

Bringing a dash of club culture to deepest Bur Dubai, *Velvet Underground* serves up an eclectic mix of music ranging from hip-hop and r'n'b through to Bollywood, Arabic and African. Free before midnight, after which men pay 100dh.

Deira

North of the Creek lies Deira, the second of the old city's two principal districts, founded in 1841, when settlers from Bur Dubai crossed the Creek to establish a new village here. Deira rapidly overtook its older neighbour in commercial importance and remains notably more built-up and cosmopolitan than Bur Dubai, with a heady ethnic mix of Emiratis, Gulf Arabs, Iranians, Indians, Pakistanis and Somalis thronging its packed streets. Specific tourist attractions are thinner on the ground here than in Bur Dubai, but the district remains the best place in Dubai for aimless wandering, and even the shortest exploration will uncover a kaleidoscopic jumble of cultures, from Indian curry houses and Iranian grocers to Somali shisha-cafés and backstreet mosques – not to mention an endless array of shops selling everything from formal black *abbeya* to belly-dancing costumes.

GOLD SOUK

Between Sikkat al Khail Rd and Old Baladiya Rd. Al Ras metro. Most shops open around 10am–10pm. MAP P.44, POCKET MAP N11

Deira's famous **Gold Souk** is usually the first stop for visitors to the district, with over three hundred shops lined up along

GOLD SOUK

its wooden-roofed main arcade, their windows packed with a staggering quantity of jewellery – it's been estimated that there are usually around ten tonnes of gold here at any one time. The souk's main attraction is price: the gold available here is among the cheapest in the world, and massive competition keeps prices keen. Though the gold industry in Dubai is carefully regulated, with the daily gold price fixed in all shops citywide, you should always **bargain**. A request for "best price" or "small discount" should yield an immediate discount of around 20–25 percent, although it always pays to shop around. The jewellery on offer ranges from restrained European-style pieces to ornate Arabian creations – the traditional Emirati bracelets, fashioned from solid gold and hung in long lines in shop windows, are particularly appealing.

HERITAGE HOUSE

Old Baladiya Rd. Al Ras metro ☎ 04 226 0286. Sat–Thurs 8am–7.30pm, Fri 2.30–7.30pm. Free. MAP P.44, POCKET MAP N11

One of the city's oldest museums, the engaging **Heritage House** offers the most complete picture of everyday life in old Dubai you'll find anywhere in town. The building (originally constructed in 1890) is a classic example of a traditional Gulf mansion, with rooms arranged around a large sandy courtyard. Each of the rooms is enlivened with exhibits evoking aspects of traditional Emirati life, along with a large cast of elaborately dressed mannequins going about their daily business: drinking coffee, spinning thread, grinding spices and so on, while a couple of waxwork children look incuriously on.

AL AHMADIYA SCHOOL

AL AHMADIYA SCHOOL

Old Baladiya Rd, next to the Heritage House. Al Ras metro ☎ 04 226 0286, 🌐 bit.ly /AlAhmadiya. Sat–Thurs 8am–7.30pm, Fri 2.30–7.30pm. Free. MAP P.44, POCKET MAP N11

The **Al Ahmadiya School** is one of the city's finest surviving examples of traditional Emirati architecture, and now houses an interesting museum devoted to the educational history of the emirate. Founded in 1912 by pearl merchant Sheikh Mohammed bin Ahmed bin Dalmouk, Al Ahmadiya was the first public school in UAE, and many of the city's leaders studied here. It was also notably egalitarian – only the sons of wealthy families were expected to pay. Museum exhibits include old photos and the inevitable mannequins, including three tiny pupils being instructed by a rather irritable-looking teacher brandishing a wooden cane.

GRAND SOUK DEIRA

Between Al Ras and Baniyas roads. Al Ras metro. Most shops open around 10am–10pm, although some may close around 1–4/5pm, and also on Fri mornings. MAP P.44, POCKET MAP N11

The extensive covered souk formerly known as Al Souk al Kabeer ("The Big Souk") was once the largest and most important market in Deira. Now rechristened **Grand Souk Deira**, the whole area has recently been given a major makeover, although most of the shops remain rather dull. Easily the most interesting part of the souk is the diminutive **Spice Souk** (signed "Herbs Market"), perhaps the most atmospheric – and certainly the most fragrant – of the city's many bazaars. Run almost exclusively by Iranian traders, the shops here stock a wide variety of culinary, medicinal and cosmetic products, with tubs of exotic merchandise set out in front of each tiny shopfront. The souk is particularly famous for its frankincense.

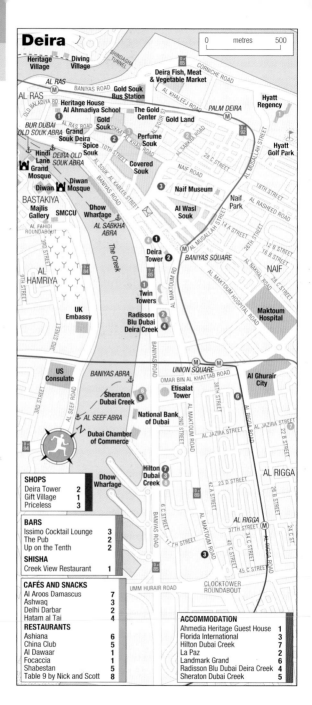

Deira

| 0 | metres | 500 |

SHOPS
Deira Tower	2
Gift Village	1
Priceless	3

BARS
Issimo Cocktail Lounge	3
The Pub	2
Up on the Tenth	2

SHISHA
| Creek View Restaurant | 1 |

CAFÉS AND SNACKS
Al Aroos Damascus	7
Ashwaq	3
Delhi Darbar	2
Hatam al Tai	4

RESTAURANTS
Ashiana	6
China Club	5
Al Dawaar	1
Focaccia	3
Shabestan	5
Table 9 by Nick and Scott	8

ACCOMMODATION
Ahmedia Heritage Guest House	1
Florida International	3
Hilton Dubai Creek	7
La Paz	2
Landmark Grand	6
Radisson Blu Dubai Deira Creek	4
Sheraton Dubai Creek	5

DHOW WHARFAGE

Deira creekside, between Deira Old Souk and Al Sabkha abra stations. Al Ras metro.
MAP P.44, POCKET MAP N12

The **Dhow Wharfage** offers a fascinating glimpse into the maritime traditions of old Dubai. At any one time, it's home to dozens of beautiful wooden dhows which berth here to load and unload cargo; hence the great tarpaulin-covered mounds of merchandise lying stacked up along the waterfront. The dhows themselves range in size from the fairly modest vessels employed for short hops up and down the coast to the large ocean-going craft used to transport goods around the Gulf and over to Iran, and even as far afield as Somalia, Pakistan and India. Virtually all of them fly the UAE flag, although they're generally manned by foreign crews who live on board.

PERFUME SOUK

Sikkat al Khail Rd, immediately east of the Gold Souk. Al Ras metro. Most shops open around 10am–10pm, although some may close around 1–4/5pm, and also on Fri mornings.
MAP P.44, POCKET MAP O11

A string of stalls, mainly along Sikkat al Khail Road but also spilling on to Al Soor and Souk Seira streets, makes up the so-called **Perfume Souk**. Most places sell a mix of international brands (not necessarily genuine) along with the much heavier and more flowery oil-based *attar* perfumes favoured by local ladies. At many shops you can also create your own scents, mixing and matching from the contents of the big bottles lined up behind the counter before taking them away in chintzy little cut-glass containers, many of which are collectibles in their own right.

DHOW WHARFAGE

DEIRA FISH, MEAT AND VEGETABLE MARKET

Between Al Khaleej and Corniche roads. Palm Deira metro. No set hours, but usually busy from early in the morning until dark, or later. MAP P.44, POCKET MAP O10

The extensive **Deira Fish, Meat and Vegetable Market** occupies a large warehouse away from the hustle and bustle of central Deira; you can reach it by taking the footbridge over Al Khaleej Road opposite Gold Land shopping centre. The fruit and vegetable section features a photogenic array of stalls piled high with rambutans, mangosteens, coconuts, vast watermelons, yams and a bewildering array of dates in huge, sticky piles. The less colourful – and far more malodorous – fish section is stocked with long lines of sharks, tuna and all sorts of other piscine species right down to sardines. There's also a small but rather gory meat section tucked away at the back.

COVERED SOUK

Between Souk Deira St and Al Sabkha Rd. Al Ras metro. Shops open around 10am–10pm, although some may close around 1–4/5pm, and also on Fri mornings. MAP P.44, POCKET MAP Q11

Deira's sprawling **Covered Souk** (a misnomer, since it isn't) comprises a rather indeterminate area of small shops arranged around the maze of narrow, pedestrianized alleyways which run south from Sikkat al Khail Road down towards the Creek. Most of the shops here are Indian-run, selling colourful, low-grade cloth for women's clothes, along with large quantities of mass-produced plastic toys and cheap household goods. It's all rather down-at-heel, but makes for an interesting stroll, especially in the area at the back of the Al Sabkha bus station, the densest and busiest part of the bazaar, particularly after dark – expect to get lost at least once. The souk then continues, more or less unabated, on the far side of Al Sabkha Road, where it's known variously as the **Naif Souk** and **Al Wasl Souk**, before reaching Al Musallah Street.

COVERED SOUK

NAIF MUSEUM

Naif Police Station, Naif Fort, Sikkat al Khail Rd. Baniyas Square metro ☎ 04 226 0286, ⊛ bit.ly/NaifMuseum. Sun–Thurs 8am–2pm. Free. MAP P.44, POCKET MAP Q7

Celebrating Dubai's formidable reputation for law and order, the modest **Naif Museum** lies tucked away in a corner of the imposing Naif Fort (originally built in 1939, but restored to death in 1997). It's actually a lot less tedious than you might fear, with mildly interesting exhibits on the history of law enforcement in the emirate from the foundation of the police force in 1956 (with just six officers under a British captain) up to the present day. Exhibits include assorted old weapons and uniforms, various old photos and a trio of short films including some interesting historical footage.

THE NATIONAL BANK OF DUBAI AND AROUND

Off Baniyas Rd immediately south of the Sheraton Dubai Creek Hotel. Union metro. MAP P.44, POCKET MAP N3

Next to the Creek in the southern part of Deira you'll find several of Dubai's original modernist landmarks. Pride of place goes to the **National Bank of Dubai** building (1998), its Creek-facing side covered by an enormous, curved sheet of highly polished glass, modelled on the sail of a traditional dhow. Next to the bank sits the shorter and squatter **Dubai Chamber of Commerce** (1995), an austerely minimalist glass-clad structure which seems to have been designed using nothing but triangles, while nearby on Omar bin al Khattab Road stands the **Etisalat Tower** (1986), instantly recognizable thanks to the enormous golf ball on its roof.

AL AROOS DAMASCUS

Shops

DEIRA TOWER

Baniyas Square. Baniyas Square metro. Most shops open 10am–9pm (although many close around 2–4/5pm). MAP P.44, POCKET MAP O13

The so-called Deira Tower "Carpet Souk" comprises thirty-odd stores spread over two floors of a large office block. Stock ranges from huge, museum-quality Persian heirlooms to ghastly framed carpet pictures and other tat.

GIFT VILLAGE

Baniyas Square (next door to Hatam al Tai café). Baniyas Square metro ☎ 04 294 6858, ⊕ gift-village.com. Daily 9am–1am (closed Fri noon–3pm). MAP P.44, POCKET MAP O12

A veritable Aladdin's cave of discounted everything, from pure tat through to designer desirables, including perfumes, electronics, clothing, bags, sports equipment, household appliances and cuddly toys.

PRICELESS

Al Maktoum Rd, near Deira Clock Tower. Al Rigga metro ☎ 04 221 5444. Sat–Thurs 10am–10pm, Fri 2–10pm. MAP P.44, POCKET MAP O4

Worth the schlep for the excellent spread of top designer menswear and ladieswear – Armani, Yves Saint-Laurent, Gucci and the like – all sold at big discounts; two-thirds off label prices is standard.

Cafés and snacks

AL AROOS DAMASCUS

Al Muraqqabat Rd. Al Rigga metro ☎ 04 221 9825, ⊕ aroosdamascus.com; Daily 7am–3pm. MAP P.44, POCKET MAP O3

One of a number of lively local Middle Eastern restaurants along Al Muraqqabat Road –

Dubai's "Little Iraq" – and parallel Al Rigga Road. All the usual Lebanese mezze and grills are on offer – well cooked, reasonably priced (mains from just 20dh) and served in huge portions.

ASHWAQ

Perfume Souk, Sikkat al Khail Rd. Al Ras metro ☎ 04 226 1164. Sat–Thurs 10am–midnight, Fri 3pm–midnight. MAP P.44, POCKET MAP O11

Close to the entrance to the bustling Gold Souk, this is one of the busiest and best of Deira's various shwarma stands, with melt-in-the-mouth shwarma sandwiches (5dh) and big fruit juices (from 10dh).

DELHI DARBAR

Al Sabkha Rd. Palm Deira metro ☎ 04 235 6161, ⊕ delhi-darbar.com. Daily 9am–midnight. MAP P.44, POCKET MAP O11

Unpretentious but excellent little no-frills restaurant serving up heartwarming meat kebabs, tandooris and Mughlai-style dishes (from 22dh) along with a good selection of veg curries (from 15dh) and superb tandoori rotis at just 1.50dh a pop.

HATAM AL TAI

Just south of Baniyas Square, behind Gift Village. Baniyas Square metro ☎ 04 224 7776. Daily 6am–12.30pm. MAP P.44, POCKET MAP Q12

Bustling, no-frills café serving meaty and filling Iranian food – kebabs, stews, shwarma plates and biriyanis – at bargain prices (30–40dh). The shwarma stand outside is also good for a snack on the go.

Restaurants

ASHIANA

Sheraton Dubai Creek Hotel, Baniyas Rd. Union metro ☎ 04 207 1733. Daily 7.30–11.30pm, plus Sun–Thurs noon–3pm. MAP P.44, POCKET MAP N3

Long-running but consistently popular Indian restaurant, offering an interesting selection of modern Indo-European fusion dishes (think tandoori lamb saddle or pan-fried duck in tamarind sauce) alongside a few old-school subcontinental classics. Live music at all meals. Mains 75–125dh.

ASHIANA

CHINA CLUB

Radisson Blu Dubai Deira Creek Hotel, Baniyas Rd. Union metro ☎ 04 222 7171. Daily noon–3pm & 7–11pm. MAP P.44, POCKET MAP Q13

The best Chinese restaurant in central Dubai, offering a daily "Yum Cha" buffet (99dh/person) at lunchtimes and à la carte in the evening, with well-prepared standards along with the restaurant's signature dim sum (32–46dh) and Peking duck. Most mains 60–90dh.

AL DAWAAR

Hyatt Regency, Corniche Rd. Palm Deira metro ☎ 04 317 2222. Daily 12.30–3.30pm & 6.30pm–midnight. MAP P.44, POCKET MAP Q1

Dubai's only revolving restaurant, offering superlative city views. Food is buffet only (175dh at lunch; 235dh at dinner, excluding drinks), featuring a mix of international cuisine plus the restaurant's signature US prime ribs – not the city's greatest culinary experience, but a decent accompaniment to the head-turning vistas outside.

FOCACCIA

Hyatt Regency, Corniche Rd. Palm Deira metro ☎ 04 210 1234. Daily except Sat 7pm–midnight, also Fri brunch 12.30–4pm. MAP P.44, POCKET MAP Q1

Rambling Italian restaurant with a casual ambience and soothing Gulf views. Food features a mix of traditional and modern Italian cuisine, with a seasonally changing menu and a mix of pasta and risottos (60–75dh), plus meat and fish mains (85–120dh).

SHABESTAN

Radisson Blu Dubai Deira Creek Hotel, Baniyas Rd. Union metro ☎ 04 222 7171. Daily 12.30–3.15pm & 7.30–11.15pm (last orders). MAP P.44, POCKET MAP Q13

This posh but rather plain Iranian restaurant retains a loyal following among Emiratis and expat Iranians thanks to its huge (if pricey) *chelo* kebabs, fish stews and other Persian specialities like *baghalah polo* (slow-cooked lamb) and *zereshk polo* (baked chicken with wild berries). Mains 95–135dh.

TABLE 9 BY NICK AND SCOTT

Hilton Dubai Creek Hotel, Baniyas Rd. Al Rigga metro ☎ 04 212 7551, ✪ table9dubai .com. Daily 7pm–midnight. MAP P.44, POCKET MAP N4

Top-notch modern European fine dining with an inventive menu that ranges from classics like pork belly and sea bass with cockles through to more quirky concoctions like duck with ceps and liquorice. You can mix and match "larger" (100dh) and "smaller" (80dh), while tasting menus are 300–450dh.

ISSIMO COCKTAIL LOUNGE

Bars

ISSIMO COCKTAIL LOUNGE

Hilton Dubai Creek Hotel, Baniyas Rd. Al Rigga metro ☎ 04 227 1111. Daily noon–4pm & 6pm–1.30am. MAP P.44, POCKET MAP N4

Chic little cocktail joint with a cute boat-shaped bar and a refreshingly unposey atmosphere – and also one of the city's few non-smoking drinking holes. A good spot for an aperitif or digestif before or after a meal at *Table 9* (see above) upstairs.

THE PUB

Radisson Blu Dubai Deira Creek Hotel, Baniyas Rd. Union metro ☎ 04 222 7171. Daily noon–4pm & 6pm–midnight. MAP P.44, POCKET MAP O13

Spacious and usually fairly peaceful English-style pub, complete with the usual fake wooden bar and lots of TVs screening global sports. Happy hour (20 percent discounts) daily 6–9pm.

UP ON THE TENTH

10th floor, Radisson Blu Dubai Deira Creek Hotel, Baniyas Rd. Union metro ☎ 04 205 7033. Daily 6.30pm–3am. MAP P.44, POCKET MAP O13

With its 80s-style decor this is not the most stylish venue in Dubai but it offers just about the best Creek views to be had in the city centre. Arrive early, grab a window seat and watch the city light up. A jazz singer and pianist perform daily (except Fri) from 10pm.

Shisha

CREEK VIEW RESTAURANT

Baniyas Rd. Baniyas Square metro ☎ 04 223 3223. Daily 10am–2am. MAP P.44, POCKET MAP O13

This convivial little open-air café scores highly for its breezy creekside location and lively late-night atmosphere. It's a good place for an after-dinner smoke (with ten types of shisha at 24–26dh) and coffee, although the food (mainly mezze and kebabs) is mediocre and the music cheesier than an Edam factory.

The inner suburbs

Fringing the southern and eastern edges of the city centre – and separating it from the more modern areas beyond – is a necklace of low-key suburbs: Garhoud, Oud Metha, Karama and Satwa. South of Deira, workaday Garhoud is home to the Dubai Creek Golf Club, with its famously futuristic clubhouse, and the adjacent yacht club, where you'll find a string of attractive waterside restaurants alongside the lovely *Park Hyatt* hotel. Directly over the Creek, Oud Metha is home to the quirky Wafi complex and the lavish Khan Murjan Souk, while north of here the enjoyably downmarket suburbs of Karama and Satwa are both interesting places to get off the tourist trail and see something of local life among the city's Indian and Filipino expats, with plenty of cheap curry houses and shops selling designer fakes.

GARHOUD

Deira City Centre metro. MAP P.52, POCKET MAP N5–O7

Covering the area between the airport and the Creek, the suburb of **Garhoud** is an interesting mishmash of up- and downmarket attractions. The **Deira City Centre** mall (see p.55) is the suburb's main draw, while on the far side of Baniyas Road lies the **Dubai Creek Golf Club**, an impressive swathe of lush fairways centred on the quirky clubhouse, with its uniquely spiky white roofline echoing the shape of a dhow's sails and masts. Close by you'll find the **Dubai Creek Yacht Club**, occupying a full-size replica of a ship's bridge, with dozens of beautiful yachts moored alongside and a cluster of good restaurants lining the waterfront. Next door sits the beguiling **Park Hyatt** hotel, its

WAFI

serene white Moroccan-style buildings, topped with vivid blue-tiled domes, adding a further touch of style to the creekside hereabouts.

WAFI

Junction of Oud Metha and Sheikh Rashid roads. Dubai Healthcare City metro ☎ 04 324 4555, ⓦ wafi.com. Daily 10am–10pm (Thurs & Fri until midnight). MAP P.52, POCKET MAP L6

The wacky Egyptian-themed **Wafi** complex is a little slice of Vegas in Dubai, dotted with obelisks, pharaonic statues, random hieroglyphs and assorted miniature pyramids. The mall is home to myriad boutiques and restaurants (see p.55 & p.56). The Egyptian theme is continued in the opulent **Raffles** hotel next door, built in the form of a vast pyramid, its summit capped with glass – particularly spectacular when lit up after dark.

KHAN MURJAN SOUK

Wafi, junction of Oud Metha and Sheikh Rashid roads. Dubai Healthcare City metro ☎ 04 324 4555, ⓦ bit.ly/KhanMurjan. Daily 10am–10pm (Thurs & Fri until midnight). MAP P.52, POCKET MAP L6

Hidden away between Wafi and the *Raffles* hotel, **Khan Murjan Souk** is one of Dubai's finest "traditional" developments, allegedly modelled after the fabled fourteenth-century Khan Murjan Souk in Baghdad. The souk is divided into four sections – Egyptian, Syrian, Moroccan and Turkish (not that you can really tell the difference) – spread over two underground levels, with a lovely outdoor restaurant at its centre (see p.56) and some 125 shops selling all manner of traditional wares. It's a great (albeit pricey) place to shop, while the faux-Arabian decor is impressively done, with lavish

CREEK PARK

detailing ranging from intricately carved wooden balconies to enormous Moroccan lanterns and colourful tilework.

CREEK PARK

Riyadh Rd, between Garhoud and Maktoum bridges. Dubai Healthcare City or Oud Metha metros. Daily 8am–10pm (Thurs–Sat until 11pm). 5dh. MAP P.52, POCKET MAP M5-7

Flanking the Creek, the expansive **Creek Park** serves as one of congested central Dubai's major lungs and is a pleasant place for an idle ramble, with good views over the Creek towards the golf and yacht clubs. The park is nicest towards dusk, when the temperature falls and the place fills up a bit, although it can be eerily deserted during weekdays. It's particularly good for kids, with plenty of playgrounds and the fun **Children's City** (see p.123) to explore, as well as the **Dubai Dolphinarium** (p.123). Children (and, indeed, adults) may also be tempted by the park's **cable car**, which offers half-hour trips (25dh; children 15dh) dangling 30m up in the air.

The inner suburbs

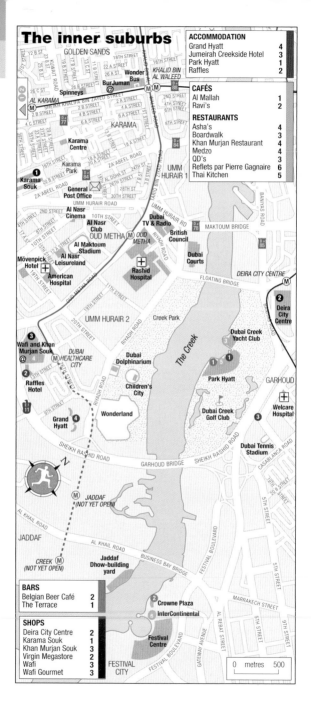

ACCOMMODATION	
Grand Hyatt	4
Jumeirah Creekside Hotel	3
Park Hyatt	1
Raffles	2

CAFÉS	
Al Mallah	1
Ravi's	2

RESTAURANTS	
Asha's	4
Boardwalk	3
Khan Murjan Restaurant	4
Medzo	4
QD's	3
Reflets par Pierre Gagnaire	6
Thai Kitchen	5

BARS	
Belgian Beer Café	2
The Terrace	1

SHOPS	
Deira City Centre	2
Karama Souk	1
Khan Murjan Souk	3
Virgin Megastore	2
Wafi	3
Wafi Gourmet	3

Shopping for fakes

Despite ongoing government clampdowns, Dubai's vibrant trade in **counterfeit goods** (bags, watches, sunglasses, pens, DVDs and so on) is still going strong. Spend any amount of time in Karama Souk, the Gold Souk or around Al Fahidi Street in Bur Dubai and you'll be repeatedly importuned with offers of "cheap copy watches" or "copy bags", as the souks' enthusiastic touts euphemistically describe them. Many fakes are still relatively expensive – you're unlikely to find bigger-ticket items for much under US$50, and plenty of items cost double that, although they'll still be a lot cheaper than the real thing. Fakes may look convincing but longevity varies considerably; some items can fall to pieces within a fortnight, and it's essential to check quality carefully – particularly stitching and zips – and be prepared to shop around and bargain like crazy.

KARAMA

Karama metro. MAP P.52, POCKET MAP L3–4

Karama is the classic Dubai inner-city suburb, home to some of the legions of Indian, Pakistani and Filipino expat workers who supply so much of the city's labour. The district is centred on **Kuwait Street** and the bustling little **Karama Centre**, with colourful shops selling *shalwar kameez* and Indian-style jewellery. At the end of Kuwait Street lies the lively **Karama Park**, surrounded by cheap and cheery Indian restaurants. South of here is the district's main tourist attraction, the **Karama Souk**, with hundreds of small shops stuffed full of fake designer clothes, watches, glasses, DVDs and other items.

SATWA

POCKET MAP H2–J2

The unpretentious district of **Satwa** is the most southerly of Dubai's predominantly low-rise, low-income inner suburbs before you reach the giant skyscrapers of Sheikh Zayed Road. It's also one of the few places in Dubai where the city's different ethnic groups really rub shoulders, reflected in an unusually eclectic selection of places to eat, from cheap-and-cheerful curry houses to Lebanese shwarma cafés and Western fast-food joints.

At the centre of the district lies **Satwa Roundabout**. The streets south of here are mainly occupied by Indian and Pakistani shops and cafés, including the well-known *Ravi's* (see p.56). West from the roundabout stretches the tree-lined **2 December Street** (formerly Al Diyafah Street), one of the nicest in Dubai – and one of the few outside the city centre with any real street life – with dozens of restaurants, and an interestingly cosmopolitan atmosphere.

KARAMA SOUK

FESTIVAL CITY

Festival Boulevard ⓦ dubaifestivalcity.com. MAP P.52, POCKET MAP M9

Festival City is one of Dubai's newest and largest purpose-built neighbourhoods – a self-contained city within a city, complete with villas and apartments, offices, golf course, marina, shopping mall and a pair of swanky five-star hotels. The centrepiece of the development is the bright, modern **Festival Centre** shopping mall: relatively small beer compared to other malls around the city, although there are fine, sweeping views from the waterfront promenade outside across the water to the dhow-building yards at Jaddaf and the long line of skyscrapers beyond.

RAS AL KHOR WILDLIFE SANCTUARY

Ras al Khor/Oud Metha roads ☎ 04 606 6822 or ☎ 04 606 6826, ⓦ wildlife.ae. Sat–Thurs 9am–4pm. Free but permits essential; apply by telephone at least two days in advance. POCKET MAP Q8

The Dubai Creek comes to an impressive end at **Ras al Khor** ("Head of the Creek"), forming an extensive inland

lagoon dotted with mangroves and surrounded by intertidal salt and mud flats – a unique area of unspoilt nature close to the city centre. The southern end of the lagoon is home to the low-key **Ras al Khor Wildlife Sanctuary**, best known for its aquatic birdlife. The sanctuary is an important stopover on winter migratory routes from East Africa to West Asia and almost seventy different species have been spotted here. It's best known for the colourful flocks of bright pink flamingoes which nest here – one of Dubai's most surreal sights when seen perched against the smoggy outlines of the city skyscrapers beyond. You can't actually go into the sanctuary, but you can birdwatch from one of three **hides** on its edge. Signage for the hides is minimal and you'll need a car to reach them, but don't expect taxi drivers to know where they are.

MEYDAN

Meydan Rd (take exit 7 off the E66 Al Ain Rd, or exit 20 of Al Khail Rd (E44), around 4km south of Ras al Khor ⓦ meydan.ae. INSIDE FRONT COVER FLAP

The vast **Meydan** complex provides conclusive proof of the ruling Maktoum family's passion – bordering on obsession – for all things equine. Founder of Godolphin, one of the world's most successful racing stables, Sheikh Mohammed's love of horses runs deep: he is said as a youth to have been able to tame wild horses considered unrideable by others. Centrepiece of the complex is the superb **racecourse**, opened in 2010 to provide a fitting venue for the **Dubai World Cup**, the world's richest horse race with a massive US$10 million in prize money.

Shops

DEIRA CITY CENTRE

Garhoud. Deira City Centre metro Ⓦdeiracity centre.com. Daily 10am–10pm (Thurs–Sat until midnight). MAP P.52, POCKET MAP O5

This big old mall remains one of the most popular in the city, with 340-plus outlets covering the whole retail spectrum, from cut-price electronics and cheap clothes through to the swanky "Jewellery Court" on Level 1, stuffed full of ultra-bling jewellery and watch shops.

KARAMA SOUK

Karama. Al Karama metro. Most shops open daily 10am–10pm. MAP P.52, POCKET MAP L4

The best place to find fake designer gear, with dozens of shops stacked full of imitation designer clothing and bags and "genuine fake watches". There are also a few low-grade souvenir shops dotted around the souk selling kitsch classics like miniature Burj al Arabs moulded in glass.

KHAN MURJAN SOUK

Wafi, Oud Metha. Dubai Healthcare City metro Ⓦwafi.com/souk-in-dubai. Sat–Wed 10am–10pm, Thurs & Fri 10am–midnight. MAP P.52, POCKET MAP L6

The hundred-plus stores in this superb replica souk (see p.51) comprise the city's best and most upmarket array of traditional crafts shops selling just about every kind of Arabian geegaw, artefact and antique you can think of.

VIRGIN MEGASTORE

Deira City Centre. Deira City Centre metro ☎04 295 8599, Ⓦvirginmegastore.me. Daily 10am–10pm (Thurs–Sat until midnight). MAP P.52, POCKET MAP O5

Dubai offshoot of the now defunct UK chain selling a great selection of Arabic pop and other genres from Morocco to

KHAN MURJAN SOUK

Iraq, as well as recordings by many Gulf and Emirati musicians. Other branches at Dubai Mall, Mercato, Mall of the Emirates and The Walk at Jumeirah Beach Residence.

WAFI

Oud Metha. Dubai Healthcare City metro Ⓦwaficity.com. Daily 10am–10pm (Thurs & Fri until midnight). MAP P.52, POCKET MAP L6

This zany Egyptian-themed mall makes for a pleasantly superior shopping experience, with a particularly good choice of independent ladies' fashion. Outlets include Ginger & Lace (funky ladieswear from international designers), the over-the-top Valleydez and the more understated By Malene Berger, showcasing work by the leading Danish designer.

WAFI GOURMET

Wafi, Oud Metha. Dubai Healthcare City metro ☎04 327 9940, Ⓦwafigourmet.com. Daily 10am–10pm (Thurs & Fri until midnight). MAP P.52, POCKET MAP L6

The ultimate Dubai deli, piled high with tempting Middle Eastern items, including big buckets of olives, nuts, spices and dried fruits, and trays of date rolls, baklava and fine chocolates.

Cafés

AL MALLAH

Al Diyafah St. Al Jafiliya metro
☎ 04 398 4962. Daily 7am–3am.
POCKET MAP J2

A classic slice of Satwa nightlife, this no-frills Lebanese café churns out good shwarmas, grills and other Middle Eastern food at bargain prices (mezze around 10dh, mains around 30dh) to a lively local crowd; the pavement terrace is a great place to people-watch.

RAVI'S

Satwa Rd, just south of Satwa Roundabout. Al Jafiliya metro. Daily 5am–3am.
POCKET MAP J2

This famous little Pakistani café, located between the copycat *Ravi Palace* and *Rawi Palace* restaurants, attracts a loyal local and expat clientele thanks to its tasty and inexpensive array of subcontinental standards (mains 15–20dh). The interior is usually packed, and it's more fun (despite the traffic) to sit out on the pavement and watch the street life of Satwa drift by.

RAVI'S

Restaurants

ASHA'S

Wafi, Oud Metha. Dubai Healthcare City metro ☎ 04 324 4100, ⓦ ashasrestaurants.com. Daily 12.30–3pm & 7pm–midnight.
MAP P.52, POCKET MAP L6

Named after legendary Bollywood chanteuse Asha Bhosle, with sleek modern orange decor and an interesting menu featuring traditional North Indian classics alongside recipes from Bhosle's own family cookbook. Mains 70–95dh.

BOARDWALK

Dubai Creek Yacht Club, Garhoud. Deira City Centre metro ☎ 04 295 6000, ⓦ dubaigolf.com/dubai-creek-golf-yacht-club. Daily noon–12.30am, Fri & Sat 8am–12.30am.
MAP P.52, POCKET MAP N6

Unpretentious, always busy restaurant on the yacht club's creekside boardwalk, with stunning city views and an eclectic range of international meat and seafood dishes (mains 60–90dh), plus a good wine list.

KHAN MURJAN RESTAURANT

Souk Khan Murjan, Wafi, Oud Metha. Dubai Healthcare City metro ☎ 04 327 9795. Daily 10am–1am. MAP P.52, POCKET MAP L6

The centrepiece of the spectacular Souk Khan Murjan, this beautiful courtyard restaurant has proved a big hit with the city's Emiratis and expat Arabs, thanks to the traditional atmosphere and unusually wide-ranging menu, featuring tempting selections from assorted Middle Eastern cuisines. Mains from around 70dh.

MEDZO

Wafi, Oud Metha. Dubai Healthcare City metro ☎ 04 324 4100, ⓦ pyramidsrestaurantsatwafi.com. Daily 12.30–3pm & 7–11.30pm. MAP P.52, POCKET MAP L6

Suave little restaurant with a cosy old-school European-style

Atlantic lobster to wild pigeon – backed up by heaps of luscious little *amuses-bouches*. The service is super-smooth, and there's a spectacular wine list, too. It's seriously expensive, though – expect to pay around 2000dh/person.

THAI KITCHEN

Park Hyatt Hotel, Garhoud. Deira City Centre metro ☎ 04 602 1818. Daily 7pm–midnight, plus Fri brunch 12.30–4pm. MAP P.52, POCKET MAP N6

Occupying part of the *Park Hyatt's* lovely creekside terrace, this superb restaurant offers all the usual Thai classics alongside a few more unusual regional specialities. Food is served in small, tapas-sized portions (35–55dh), meaning that you can sample a wide range of dishes and flavours.

dining room and a good selection of Italian-cum-Mediterranean cuisine – pastas, pizzas and risottos (65–75dh) alongside bigger meat and seafood mains (from 100dh).

QD'S

Dubai Creek Yacht Club, Garhoud. Deira City Centre metro ☎ 04 295 6000, ⓦ dubaigolf .com/dubai-creek-golf-yacht-club. Daily 5pm–2am. MAP P.52, POCKET MAP N6

Fun and good-value restaurant-cum-bar-cum-shisha café in a superb location on a large open-air terrace overlooking the Creek. The cheap and cheerful pub-grub-style menu features lots of pizzas and Lebanese kebabs (mains from around 50dh), and there's also a big selection of shisha and a well-stocked bar.

REFLETS PAR PIERRE GAGNAIRE

InterContinental Hotel, off Crescent Drive ☎ 04 701 1111, ⓦ facebook.com /refletsparpierregagnaire. Daily 7–11.30pm. MAP P.52, POCKET MAP M9

One of the city's top European fine-dining experiences, showcasing French chef Pierre Gagnaire's innovative modern French cuisine. The short menu features a mix of regularly changing meat and seafood creations – anything from blue

Bars

BELGIAN BEER CAFÉ

Crowne Plaza Hotel, Festival City ☎ 04 701 2222, ⓦ facebook.com/belgian beercafedubai. Daily noon–2am (Fri & Sat until 3am). MAP P.52, POCKET MAP M9

Convivial Belgian-style pub-cum-restaurant, with an eye-catching traditional wooden interior, an excellent range of speciality beers on tap or by the bottle (including draught Hoegaarden, Leffe and Belle-Vue Kriek) and good traditional Flemish cooking.

THE TERRACE

Park Hyatt Hotel, Garhoud. Deira City Centre metro ☎ 04 602 1234, ⓦ dubai.park.hyatt .com. Daily noon–2am. MAP P.52, POCKET MAP N6

Seductive (if pricey) waterside bar, with seating either indoors or out on the terrace over-looking the Creek. The mellow and romantic mood is helped along by smooth chill-out music and a nice selection of cocktails and other tipples.

Sheikh Zayed Road and Downtown Dubai

Around 5km south of the Creek, the upwardly mobile suburbs of southern Dubai begin in spectacular style with the massed skyscrapers of Sheikh Zayed Road and the huge Downtown Dubai development: an extraordinary sequence of neck-cricking high-rises which march south from the landmark Emirates Towers to the cloud-capped Burj Khalifa, the world's tallest building. This is the modern city at its most futuristic and flamboyant, and perhaps the defining example of Dubai's insatiable desire to offer more luxury, more glitz and more retail opportunities than the competition, with a string of record-breaking attractions which now include not just the world's tallest building but also its largest mall, tallest hotel and biggest fountain.

EMIRATES TOWERS

Sheikh Zayed Rd. Emirates Towers metro ⓦ bit.ly/JEThotel. MAP P.60, POCKET MAP G4

Opened in 2000, the soaring **Emirates Towers** remain one of modern Dubai's the most iconic symbols, despite increasing competition from newer and even more massive landmarks. The larger office tower (355m) was the tallest building in the Middle East and tenth highest in the world when it was completed, though now it barely scrapes into the top ten tallest buildings in the city.

The taller tower houses the offices of Emirates airlines; the smaller is occupied by the exclusive *Jumeirah Emirates Towers* hotel (see p.107). The office tower isn't open to the public, but there are plenty of

opportunities to look around the hotel tower, most spectacularly from the 50th- and 51st-floor *Vu's* bar and restaurant (see p.67 & p.65).

DUBAI INTERNATIONAL FINANCIAL CENTRE

Between Sheikh Zayed Rd and 312 Rd. Emirates Tower or Financial Centre metros ⓦ difc.ae. MAP P.60, POCKET MAP G4

The **Dubai International Financial Centre (DIFC)** is the city's financial hub and home to myriad banks, investment companies and other enterprises. The DIFC's northern end is marked by **The Gate**, a striking building looking like a kind of postmodern Arc de Triomphe-cum-office block. The Gate is surrounded on three sides by further buildings linked by "The Balcony", an attractive raised terrace lined with assorted cafés and shops. Off on the east side of the complex is the **Gate Village**, now one of the focal points of Dubai's burgeoning visual arts scene, with virtually every building occupied by assorted galleries.

DUBAI WORLD TRADE CENTRE

Sheikh Zayed Rd, by Trade Centre Roundabout. World Trade Centre metro ⓦ dwtc.com. MAP P.60, POCKET MAP J4

On the north side of the sprawling **Dubai International Convention and Exhibition Centre** rises the venerable old **Dubai World Trade Centre** tower, Dubai's first skyscraper. Commissioned in 1979 by the visionary Sheikh Rashid, then ruler of Dubai, this 39-storey edifice was widely regarded as a massive white elephant when it was first built, standing as it did in the middle of what was then empty desert far from the old city centre. Contrary to expectations it proved an enormous success, serving as an important anchor for future development along the strip and fully justifying Sheikh Rashid's far-sighted ambition.

ALONG SHEIKH ZAYED ROAD

MAP P.60, POCKET MAP F4–H4

A more or less unbroken line of high-rises lines Sheikh Zayed Road south of the Emirates Towers. Heading down the strip brings you almost immediately to the daft **Al Yaqoub Tower**: effectively a postmodern replica of London's Big Ben, although at 330m it's well over three times the height of the 96m-tall UK landmark.

Continuing down the road brings you to the graceful **Rose Rayhaan**, at 333m formerly the world's tallest hotel until the recent opening of the new *JW Marriott Marquis Dubai* in nearby Business Bay, while slightly further south the strip reaches a suitably dramatic end with the iconic **Dusit Thani** hotel, a towering glass-and-metal edifice inspired by the traditional Thai *wai*, a prayer-like gesture of welcome, though it looks more like a huge upended tuning fork thrust into the ground.

AL YAQOUB TOWER

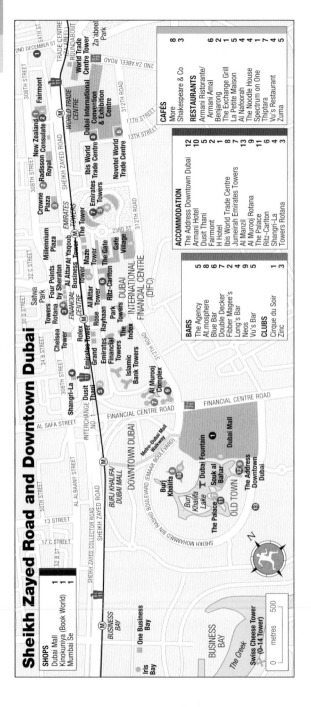

Sheikh Zayed Road and Downtown Dubai

SHOPS
Dubai Mall	1
Kinokuniya (Book World)	1
Mumbai Se	1

CAFÉS
More	8
Shakespeare & Co	3

RESTAURANTS
Armani Ristorante/	6
Armani Amal	2
Benjarong	1
The Exchange Grill	5
La Petite Maison	4
Al Nafoorah	4
The Noodle House	7
Spectrum on One	1
Thiptara	4
Vu's Restaurant	5
Zuma	

ACCOMMODATION
The Address Downtown Dubai	12
Armani Hotel	10
Dusit Thani	5
Fairmont	2
H Hotel	1
Ibis World Trade Centre	8
Jumeirah Emirates Towers	7
Al Manzil	13
Al Murooj Rotana	9
The Palace	11
Ritz-Carlton	6
Shangri-La	4
Towers Rotana	3

BARS
The Agency	5
At.mosphere	8
Blue Bar	6
Double Decker	7
Fibber Magee's	2
Long's Bar	4
Neos	9
Vu's Bar	5

CLUBS
Cirque du Soir	1
Zinc	3

BURJ KHALIFA

Sheikh Mohammed bin Rashid Blvd (Emaar Blvd), Downtown Dubai. Burj Khalifa/Dubai Mall metro ☎ 04 888 8888, ⓦ burjkhalifa.ae. At the Top tours depart from the ticket desk in the lower-ground floor of the Dubai Mall (Sun–Wed 9am–midnight, Thurs 8.30am–midnight, Fri & Sat 4.30pm–midnight; tickets pre-booked online 100dh, immediate entry tickets 400dh). MAP P.60, POCKET MAP E4

Rising imperiously skywards at the southern end of Sheikh Zayed Road stands the needle-thin **Burj Khalifa**, the world's tallest building. Opened in early 2010 after five years' intensive construction, the Burj finally topped out at a staggering 828m, comprehensively smashing all existing world records. The astonishing scale of the Burj is difficult to fully comprehend – the building is best appreciated at a distance, from where you can properly appreciate its jaw-dropping height. Most of the tower is occupied by some 900 residential apartments; lower floors are occupied by the world's first **Armani hotel** (see p.106).

Access to the Burj Khalifa is strictly controlled. Most visitors take the expensive tour to the **"At the Top" observation deck** (on floor 124) for sensational views over the city. The tour also includes some interesting displays on the creation of the tower, although you should expect large crowds and long queues whenever you visit.

DUBAI MALL

Financial Centre Rd. Burj Khalifa/Dubai Mall metro ⓦ thedubaimall.com. Daily 10am–10pm, Thurs–Sat until midnight. MAP P.60, POCKET MAP E5–F5

Right next to the Burj Khalifa is the supersized **Dubai Mall**, with over 1200 shops spread across four floors and covering over a million square metres –

THE WATERFALL, DUBAI MALL

making it easily the largest mall in the world measured by total area. Just about every retail chain in the city has an outlet here. Look out too for the eye-catching **The Waterfall**, complete with life-size statues of fibreglass divers, which cascades from the top of the mall down to the bottom, four storeys below.

DUBAI AQUARIUM AND UNDERWATER ZOO

Financial Centre Rd. Burj Khalifa/Dubai Mall metro ☎ 04 448 5200, ⓦ thedubaiaquarium .com. Sun–Wed 10am–10pm, Thurs–Sat 10am–midnight. 80dh. MAP P.60, POCKET MAP F5

Assuming you enter the Dubai Mall's main entrance off Financial Centre Road, one of the first things you'll see is the spectacular viewing panel of the **Dubai Aquarium and Underwater Zoo**: a huge transparent floor-to-ceiling aquarium filled to the brim with fish large and small, including sand-tiger sharks, stingrays, and some large and spectacularly ugly grouper. The **Underwater Zoo** upstairs is relatively unexciting compared to the enormous tank, and more likely to appeal to children than to adults.

DUBAI FOUNTAIN

Burj Khalifa Lake, Downtown Dubai. Burj Khalifa/Dubai Mall metro ☎04 362 7500, ✆bit.ly/TheDubaiFountain. Displays daily at 1pm & 1.30pm and then every 30min 6–11pm (Thurs–Sat until 11.30pm). MAP P.60. POCKET MAP E5

Winding through the heart of Downtown Dubai is the large **Burj Khalifa Lake**, a section of which doubles as the spectacular 275m-long **Dubai Fountain**, the world's biggest, capable of shooting jets of water up to 150m high, and illuminated with over 6000 lights and 25 colour projectors. The fountain really comes to life after dark, spouting carefully choreographed watery flourishes which "dance" elegantly in time to a range of Arabic, Hindi and classical songs, viewable from anywhere around the lake for free.

OLD TOWN

Burj Khalifa/Dubai Mall metro. Souk Al Bahar Sat–Thurs 10am–10pm, Fri 2–10pm MAP P.60. POCKET MAP E5

The chintzy **Old Town** development, across the lake from the Burj Khalifa, is a low-rise sprawl of sand-coloured buildings with traditional Moorish styling. Centrepiece of the development is the **Souk al Bahar**, a small, Arabian-themed mall, although it feels rather underpowered after the excesses of the neighbouring Dubai Mall. A string of restaurants lines the waterfront terrace outside, offering peerless views of Burj Khalifa.

BUSINESS BAY

Business Bay metro. MAP P.60. POCKET MAP C4–D5

Dubai's last big hurrah before the credit crunch hit town in 2008, the vast **Business Bay** development was originally intended to comprise a swanky new high-rise district around an extension of the Creek, although the entire scheme has got stuck in limbo. A few completed buildings are worth a look, however. Close to the metro, the **JW Marriott Marquis Dubai** is currently the tallest hotel in the world at a cool 355m, while opposite the *Marriott* stands the extraordinary crescent-shaped **Iris Bay** building (still not quite finished). Further down the road, you can't fail to notice the funky O-14 building, popularly known as the **Swiss Cheese Tower** thanks to the undulating layer of white cladding that envelops the entire structure, dotted with around 1300 circular holes and looking uncannily like an enormous piece of postmodern Emmenthal cheese.

DUBAI FOUNTAIN

Shops

DUBAI MALL

Downtown Dubai. Burj Khalifa/Dubai Mall metro ⓦthedubaimall.com. Daily 10am–10pm (Thurs–Sat until midnight). MAP P.60, POCKET MAP E5–F5

Highlights in this mother of all malls include the flagship Bloomingdale's and Galeries Lafayette department stores; "Fashion Avenue", home to the biggest array of designer labels in Dubai; and the attractively chintzy "Souk" area, with a further 120 shops selling gold, jewellery and Arabian perfumes. Upstairs you'll find a Dubai branch of Hamleys, the famous London toyshop; Não do Brasil, an eye-catching shop stuffed full of funky trainers; and Kinokuniya (see below).

KINOKUNIYA (BOOK WORLD)

Second floor, Dubai Mall. Burj Khalifa/Dubai Mall metro ⓣ 04 434 0111, ⓦkinokuniya .com/ae. Daily 10am–10pm (Thurs–Sat until midnight). MAP P.60, POCKET MAP E5

This local outpost of the famous Japanese chain is far and away Dubai's best bookshop – a vast emporium stuffed with a simply massive array of titles, ranging from mainstream novels, travel guides and magazines through to graphic novels and a brilliant manga selection.

MUMBAI SE

Dubai Mall. Burj Khalifa/Dubai Mall metro ⓣ 04 434 0626, ⓦfacebook.com /mumbaiseuae. Daily 10am–10pm (Thurs–Sat until midnight). MAP P.60, POCKET MAP E5

Top-end designer Indian fashions (ladieswear only) at prices to match – the place to go if you want to feel like Bollywood royalty. Other branches at the Festival Centre and Marina Mall.

DUBAI MALL SOUK

Cafés

MORE

Dubai Mall. Burj Khalifa/Dubai Mall metro ⓣ 04 339 8934, ⓦ morecafe.biz. Daily 8am–11pm. MAP P.60, POCKET MAP E5

With a big terrace overlooking the Dubai Fountain and Burj Khalifa, the Dubai Mall branch of this citywide chain of attractive European-style cafés is a good place either for breakfast, lunch, a light dinner or just a cup of superior coffee. The menu features moreish sandwiches and home-made pasta (45–60dh) plus an eclectic selection of international mains (55–80dh). Free wi-fi.

SHAKESPEARE & CO

South side of Al Attar Business Tower, 37th St, off Sheikh Zayed Rd, roughly opposite the Ritz-Carlton Hotel. Financial Centre metro ⓣ 04 331 1757, ⓦ shakespeareandco .ae. Daily 7am–1am. MAP P.60, POCKET MAP G4

The original branch of a citywide café-cum-coffee shop chain, characterized by its distinctively chintzy decor – a kind of high-camp Victoriana, usually with cherubs. Food includes a wide selection of soups, salads, sandwiches and crêpes (from 35dh), plus more substantial mains.

Restaurants

ARMANI RISTORANTE/ARMANI AMAL

Burj Khalifa. Burj Khalifa/Dubai Mall metro ☏ 04 888 3888, ⓦ dubai.armanihotels.com. Daily 7–11.30pm. MAP P.60, POCKET MAP E4

Top of the tree among the culinary options at the new *Armani* hotel is the signature *Armani Ristorante*, serving fine-dining regional Italian cuisine (mains 140–290dh), particularly Tuscan dishes. The hotel's *Armani Amal* restaurant also gets good reviews for its inventive regional Indian cuisine with a European twist (mains 130–180dh). Note that if you're not staying at the hotel you'll need an advance reservation to gain admittance.

BENJARONG

Dusit Thani Hotel, Sheikh Zayed Rd. Financial Centre metro ☏ 04 317 4515. Daily noon–3pm & 7–10.30pm (last orders). MAP P.60, POCKET MAP F4

Set in a delicately painted wooden pavilion on the 24th floor of the *Dusit Thani*, *Benjarong* offers some of the best Royal Thai cooking in Dubai. There's a particularly good selection of fish and

BENJARONG

seafood, plus the usual meat stir-fries and red and yellow curries, and they also do a lively Friday brunch. Most mains 55–75dh.

THE EXCHANGE GRILL

Fairmont Hotel, Sheikh Zayed Rd. World Trade Centre metro ☏ 04 311 8559, ⓦ fairmont.com. Daily 7pm–midnight. MAP P.60, POCKET MAP H3

This small and rather exclusive steakhouse has just fourteen tables with huge leather armchairs for seating, and a menu of Premium Gold Angus and Wagyu cuts (215–295dh) plus a few upmarket seafood dishes and an extensive wine list.

LA PETITE MAISON

Building 8, The Gate, DIFC. Emirates Towers metro ☏ 04 439 0505, ⓦ lpmdubai.ae. Daily noon–3.30pm & 7–11.30pm. MAP P.60, POCKET MAP G4

An offshoot of the famous Nice restaurant, this is as authentic as French restaurants come in the UAE, offering traditional *cuisine niçoise* in a bright white dining room which feels intimate and pleasantly formal but not too stuffy. The excellent cooking blends Gallic haute cuisine with a dash of Mediterranean zing, with most mains 120–200dh. Reservations usually essential.

AL NAFOORAH

Emirates Towers Boulevard. Emirates Towers metro ☏ 04 330 0000. Daily 12.30–3pm (Fri & Sat from 1pm) & 7–11pm. MAP P.60, POCKET MAP G4

One of the city's best places for Middle Eastern food, *Al Nafoorah* looks more like a slightly starchy Parisian establishment than a traditional Lebanese restaurant. What's on offer is the real deal, however, from the superb array of mezze through to the perfectly cooked selection of fish, meat grills and kebabs. Mezze from 30dh, mains from 60dh.

THE NOODLE HOUSE

Emirates Towers Boulevard. Emirates Towers metro ☎ 04 319 8757, ⊛ thenoodlehouse.com. Daily noon–11.30pm. MAP P.60, POCKET MAP G4

A Dubai institution, this cheapish and very cheerful noodle bar caters to an endless stream of diners who huddle up on long communal tables to refuel on excellent Chinese and southeast Asian food. No reservations, so you might have to queue at busy times. Most mains around 60dh.

SPECTRUM ON ONE

Fairmont Hotel, Sheikh Zayed Rd. World Trade Centre metro ☎ 04 311 8101, ⊛ fairmont.com. Daily 6.30pm–12.30am (last orders), plus Fri noon–3pm. MAP P.60, POCKET MAP H3

This good-looking modern restaurant has no fewer than seven separate kitchens, each specializing in a different cuisine, so you can mix and match from Arabian, Indian, Chinese, Japanese, Thai, European and seafood menus as you fancy – very typical of Dubai's more-is-more approach to life, although the food is actually pretty good. Most mains 100–150dh.

THIPTARA

The Palace Hotel, Old Town. Burj Khalifa/ Dubai Mall metro ☎ 04 428 7961, ⊛ theaddress.com/en/dining/thiptara. Daily 7–11.30pm. MAP P.60, POCKET MAP E5

This beautiful Thai restaurant offers probably the best night-time view of the Burj Khalifa and Dubai Fountain. The menu is strongest on seafood, but also offers a fair spread of meat dishes (though few veg options). Most mains 90–150dh. Reservations recommended.

THIPTARA

VU'S RESTAURANT

50th floor, Jumeirah Emirates Towers Hotel, Sheikh Zayed Rd. Emirates Towers metro ☎ 04 319 8088, ⊛ jumeirah.com. Sun–Thurs 12.30–3pm & 7.30pm–midnight, plus Fri 7.30pm–midnight. MAP P.60, POCKET MAP G4

At the city's second-highest restaurant the view is not surprisingly a main draw, though *Vu's* is also one of the city's top fine-dining venues, with a short but sophisticated menu of modern European cuisine. Mains from 200dh.

ZUMA

Gate Village, Building 6. Emirates Towers metro ☎ 04 425 5660, ⊛ zumarestaurant .com. Daily: restaurant 12.30–2.45pm (last orders) & 7pm–1am (Thurs & Fri until 2am); bar 12.30pm–1 or 2am. MAP P.60, POCKET MAP G4

Very hip new Japanese bar-restaurant with a dining area (including sushi counter and *robata* grill) downstairs, and a bar-lounge above. Informal *izakaya*-style dining – with shared dishes served in no particular sequence – is the order of the day, although the food itself is top-notch (as are the prices). Mains 80–165dh; express lunch menu 80dh. DJs nightly from around 9pm. Reservations usually essential.

Bars

THE AGENCY

Emirates Towers Boulevard shopping
complex. Emirates Towers metro ☎ 04 319
8741. Daily noon–1am (Fri & Sat until
midnight only). MAP P.60, POCKET MAP G4

Sedate-looking wood-panelled
wine bar serving up a decent
selection of vintages from all
the world's major wine-
producing countries by the
glass or bottle, plus assorted
champagnes, cocktails
and beers.

AT.MOSPHERE

Burj Khalifa ☎ 04 888 3444,
🌐 atmosphereburjkhalifa.com. Bar daily
noon–2am. MAP P.60, POCKET MAP E4

At.mosphere's selling point
couldn't be simpler: this is the
world's highest bar and
restaurant, located almost half
a kilometre above ground level
on the 122nd floor of the
world's tallest building. Decor
is svelte and modern, although
your eyes will inevitably be
drawn to the huge views
outside. There's a minimum
spend of 200dh if you want to
visit the bar – where they also
do light meals and pricey
afternoon teas (290dh). If you
want to go the whole hog, the
attached restaurant offers
upmarket international meat
and seafood dishes (mains
260–360dh), although at these
prices you're probably better off
heading to one of the Armani
restaurants downstairs.

BLUE BAR

Novotel, World Trade Centre. World Trade
Centre metro ☎ 04 332 0000, 🌐 facebook
.com (search for "Blue Bar Dubai"). Daily
2pm–2am. MAP P.60, POCKET MAP H4

This stylish little bar is a
pleasant spot for a mellow
drink earlier in the evening,
with a sedate crowd and a good

BLUE BAR

selection of speciality Belgian
beers, plus cocktails, wines,
premium whiskies and superior
bar meals. Things can get lively
later on in the evening from
Thursday to Saturday when
there's a live band playing a mix
of blues, jazz, classic rock and
pop (from around 9.30pm until
1am). Happy hour daily 6–8pm
(buy one get one free).

DOUBLE DECKER

Al Murooj Rotana Hotel, Financial Centre Rd.
Financial Centre metro 🌐 rotana.com
/almuroojrotana. Daily noon–3am. MAP P.60,
POCKET MAP F4

One of the liveliest pubs in
town, with quirky decor
themed after the old London
Routemaster buses and usually
busy with a fairly tanked-up
crowd of expats and Western
tourists. Live music every
Friday, and a DJ from around
9pm the rest of the week.

FIBBER MAGEE'S

Off Sheikh Zayed Rd. Emirates Towers metro
☎ 04 332 2400, 🌐 fibbersdubai.com. Daily
noon–2.30am (last orders). MAP P.60,
POCKET MAP H3

One of the city's best-kept
secrets, and probably Dubai's
most impressive stab at a

traditional European pub, with a spacious, very nicely done out wood-beamed interior and a good selection of draught beers including Kilkenny, Guinness, London Pride and Peroni, plus Magners cider. There's also regular live music and good, homely pub food. To reach it, go down the small side road between *Jashan* restaurant and *Zoom* (just south of the *Radisson* hotel) and it's on your left in the bottom of the *Stables* restaurant building.

LONG'S BAR

Towers Rotana Hotel, Sheikh Zayed Rd. Financial Centre metro ☎ 04 312 2202, ⓦ rotana.com/towersrotana. Daily noon–3am. MAP P.60, POCKET MAP G3

Proud home to the longest bar in the Middle East, this English-style pub offers one of the strip's more convivial and downmarket drinking holes, with all the usual tipples and the ubiquitous TV sports.

NEOS

63rd floor, The Address Downtown Dubai Hotel, Sheikh Mohammed bin Rashid Blvd (Emaar Boulevard). Burj Khalifa/Dubai Mall metro ☎ 04 436 8888, ⓦ theaddress.com. Daily 6pm–3am. MAP P.60, POCKET MAP E5

The second-highest bar in Dubai (eclipsed only by *At.mosphere*), with great views over the Downtown Dubai and the Burj Khalifa – although the overblown decor, smoky atmosphere, ostentatious crowd and steep prices may leave you shaken rather than stirred.

VU'S BAR

51st floor, Jumeirah Emirates Towers Hotel, Sheikh Zayed Rd. Emirates Towers metro ☎ 04 319 8088, ⓦ jumeirah.com. Daily 6pm–3am. MAP P.60, POCKET MAP G4

One of the highest licensed perches in Dubai, with floor-to-ceiling windows on one side through which to enjoy the spectacular views and a vast selection of predictably pricey drinks (beer bottles 40dh, cocktails from 55dh, wines from 62dh).

Clubs

CIRQUE DU SOIR

Fairmont Hotel, Sheikh Zayed Rd. World Trade Centre metro ☎ 056 115 4507, ⓦ cirquedusoirdubai.com. Mon, Tues, Thurs & Fri 10.30pm–3am. MAP P.60, POCKET MAP H3

An offshoot of the original London club, this top-end venue is half club, half music hall, with big-top-inspired decor and assorted performers including burlesque podium dancers, kooky clowns and juggling waiters.

ZINC

Crowne Plaza Hotel, Sheikh Zayed Rd. Emirates Towers metro ☎ 050 151 5609, ⓦ facebook.com/zincnightclub. Daily 10pm–3am. Entrance 100dh Thurs–Sun, 50dh Mon–Wed. MAP P.60, POCKET MAP G3

One of the longest-running and most enduringly popular clubs in Dubai, thanks to an eclectic soundtrack and unposey atmosphere. Music features a mix of retro, r'n'b, hip-hop and house, depending on the night.

VU'S BAR

Jumeirah

A couple of kilometres south of the Creek, the beachside suburb of Jumeirah marks the beginning of southern Dubai's endless suburban sprawl, with swathes of chintzy low-rise villas providing a home to many of the city's European expats and other upper-income residents. The suburb is strung out along the Jumeirah Road, which arrows straight down the coast and provides the area with its principal focus, lined with a long string of shopping malls; most are fairly low-key, apart from the quirky, Italian-themed Mercato. Other attractions include the traditional Jumeirah Mosque (the only one in Dubai currently accessible to non-Muslims) and the Majlis Ghorfat um al Sheif, the former summer retreat of Dubai's erstwhile ruler Sheikh Rashid, while more hedonistic diversions can be found at Jumeirah Beach Park, the city's most attractive public beach.

JUMEIRAH MOSQUE

Jumeirah Rd. Bus #8, #C10 or #X28
☎ 04 353 6666, ⊛ cultures.ae. 1hr tours Tues, Thurs, Sat & Sun at 10am. 10dh (under-5s not allowed; no pre-booking required). MAP P.69, POCKET MAP H1

Rising proudly above the northern end of the Jumeirah Road, the stately **Jumeirah Mosque** is one of the largest and most attractive in the city,

JUMEIRAH MOSQUE

built in quasi-Fatimid (Egyptian) style, with a pair of soaring minarets, a roofline embellished with delicately carved miniature domes and richly decorated windows set in elaborate rectangular recesses. As with many of Dubai's more venerable-looking buildings though, medieval appearances are deceptive – the mosque was actually built in 1979.

It also has the added attraction of being the only mosque in Dubai that non-Muslims can visit, thanks to the regular **tours** run by the Sheikh Mohammed Centre for Cultural Understanding (see p.35). These offer a good opportunity to get a look at the mosque's rather florid interior, with its distinctive green-and-orange colour scheme and delicately painted arches, although the real draw is the informative guides, who explain some of the basic precepts and practices of Islam before inviting questions.

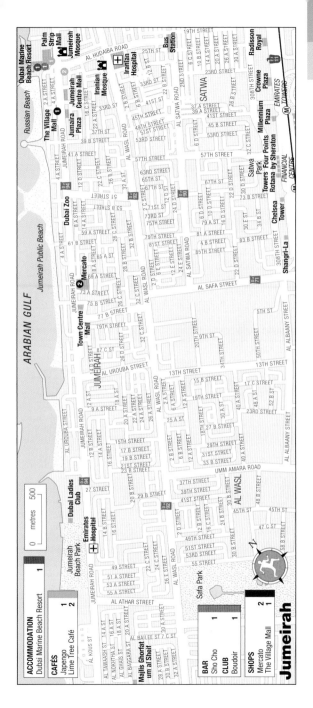

ACCOMMODATION
Dubai Marine Beach Resort   1

CAFÉS
Japengo   1
Lime Tree Café   2

Majlis Ghorfat
um al Sheif

BAR
Sho Cho   1

CLUB
Boudoir   1

SHOPS
Mercato   2
The Village Mall   1

Jumeirah

ARABIAN GULF

Jumeirah Public Beach

Russian Beach

Dubai Marine Beach Resort

Palm Strip Mall

Jumeirah Centre Mall

The Village Mall

Iranian Hospital

Iranian Mosque

Bus Station

SATWA

Jumaira Plaza

Millennium Plaza

Crowne Plaza

Radisson Royal

Towers Four Points Rotana by Sheraton

Chelsea Tower

Shangri-La

FINANCIAL CENTRE

EMIRATES TOWERS

Satwa Park

Dubai Zoo

Mercato

Town Centre Mall

JUMEIRAH

Jumeirah Beach Park

Dubai Ladies Club

Emirates Hospital

AL WASL

Safa Park

metres 500

69

DUBAI ZOO

Jumeirah Rd. Bus #8, #88, #C10 ☎ 04 349 6444 or ☎ 04 344 0462. Daily except Tues 10am–5.30pm. 2dh. MAP P.69, POCKET MAP F1

The first zoo on the Arabian peninsula when it was founded in 1967, **Dubai Zoo** serves as the overcrowded home to a wide range of animals, almost all of which arrived at the zoo having been taken from smugglers apprehended by UAE customs officials. The resultant mishmash of animals includes giraffes, tigers, lions, chimps, brown bears, Arabian wolves and oryx, plus assorted birds – although it's difficult to see very much thanks to the ugly cages, covered in thick wire mesh.

MERCATO

Jumeirah Rd. Bus #8, #88, #C10 or #X28 ⓦ mercatoshoppingmall.com. Daily 10am–10pm (Thurs–Sat until midnight). MAP P.69, POCKET MAP E1

About halfway down Jumeirah Road, the eye-popping **Mercato** mall looks like a kind of miniature medieval Italian city rebuilt by the Disney Corporation. Brightly coloured quasi-Venetian-cum-Tuscan palazzi are arranged around a huge central atrium overlooked by panoramic balconies – a memorable example of the sort of brazen kitsch that Dubai does so well.

JUMEIRAH BEACH PARK

Jumeirah Rd. Bus #8, #88, #C10 or #X28. Daily 8am–10.30pm (Thurs–Sat until 11pm); Mon ladies and boys aged up to 4 only. 5dh. MAP P.69, POCKET MAP C1

Squeezed in between the sea and Jumeirah Road near the suburb's southern end, **Jumeirah Beach Park** is easily the nicest park and public beach in Dubai. The beach itself is large enough to soak up the crowds, with a fine wide swathe of white sand manned by lifeguards and equipped with loungers and parasols, while the pleasantly wooded strip of park behind has lots of shaded grass for picnics, barbecue facilities, a couple of cafés and a well-equipped play area for kids.

MAJLIS GHORFAT UM AL SHEIF

17 St (signed off Jumeirah Road by the BinSina pharmacy; turn down 17 St for about 50m and the majlis is on your left). Bus #8, #88 or #X28 ☎ 04 852 1374. Sat–Thurs 8.30am–8.30pm, Fri 2.30–8.30pm. 1dh. MAP P.69, POCKET MAP A1

Tucked away off the southern end of Jumeirah Road, the **Majlis Ghorfat um al Sheif** offers a touching memento of old Dubai, now incongruously marooned amid a sea of modern villas. Built in 1955 when Jumeirah was no more than a small fishing village, this modest traditional house – a simple two-storey coral-and-gypsum building embellished with fine doors and window shutters made of solid teak – was formerly used by Sheikh Rashid, the inspiration behind modern Dubai's spectacular develop- ment, as a summer house.

Shops

MERCATO

Jumeirah Rd ⓦ mercatoshoppingmall.com.
Daily 10am–10pm (Fri until midnight). MAP P.69,
POCKET MAP E1

This kitsch Italian-themed mall
(see opposite) packs in a good
selection of rather upmarket
outlets aimed at affluent local
villa dwellers, including a
decent range of mainstream
designer labels.

THE VILLAGE MALL

Jumeirah Beach Rd ⓦ thevillagedubai.com.
Sat–Thurs 10am–10pm, Fri 4–10pm. MAP P.69,
POCKET MAP G1

The best of the various small
malls scattered along the
northern end of Jumeirah
Beach Road, home to the
excellent hippychick-chic
S*uce, the city's leading
independent boutique, and
another fashion store selling
the work of top Indian designer
Ayesha Depala, plus a homely
little branch of *Shakespeare &
Co* (see p.63).

Cafés

JAPENGO

Palm Strip Mall, Jumeirah Rd ⓣ 04 345
4979, ⓦ binhendi.com/v2/japengo.htm. Daily
8.30am–1am. MAP P.69, POCKET MAP H1

Bright modern café-restaurant
with one of the most
shamelessly eclectic menus in
town, based around a longish
list of Japanese standards
(sushi, sashimi, maki) spliced
together with Middle Eastern
mezze, Southeast Asian
stir-fries, plus pizzas and
pastas, sandwiches and salads.
Mains 50–80dh. Branches
citywide at BurJuman, Wafi,
Festival City, Dubai Mall, Souk
Madinat Jumeirah, Mall of the
Emirates and Ibn Battuta Mall.

LIME TREE CAFÉ

Jumeirah Rd ⓣ 04 349 8498,
ⓦ thelimetreecafe.com. Daily 7.30am–6pm.
MAP P.69, POCKET MAP H1

Eternally popular with
Jumeirah's expat wives and
ladies-who-lunch, this
cheery little establishment is
a great place to people-watch,
while food includes moreish
wraps, focaccias, panini,
quiches, salads and cakes,
plus tasty juices.

Bar

SHO CHO

Dubai Marine Beach Resort, Jumeirah Rd
ⓣ 04 346 1111, ⓦ dxbmarine.com/Sho-Cho.
Daily 7pm–2am or later (kitchen closes at
midnight). MAP P.69, POCKET MAP H1

This chic little bar-cum-
Japanese restaurant seems to
have been around forever, but
remains modestly popular
among the city's Lebanese and
Bollywood party set, despite
(or perhaps because of) the
trumped-up door staff. A
nightly DJ plays mainly house
– although the biggest night at
present is the pose-free 1980s
session every Sunday.

Club

BOUDOIR

Dubai Marine Beach Resort, Jumeirah Rd
ⓣ 04 345 5995 or ⓣ 346 1111, ⓦ myboudoir
.com. Daily 9pm–3am. MAP P.69, POCKET MAP H1

This sultry bar-cum-nightclub
looks like the apartment of an
upper-class nineteenth-century
Parisian courtesan, with plush
red drapes, chintzy chandeliers
and an indecent number of
mirrors. There's a regular DJ on
Tuesday, Thursday and Friday,
plus occasional visiting
international DJs at other
times; on others nights it's
more of a bar.

The Burj al Arab and around

Some 18km south of the Creek, the suburb of Umm Suqeim marks the beginning of Dubai's spectacular modern beachside developments, announced with a flourish by three of Dubai's most famous landmarks: the iconic sail-shaped Burj al Arab hotel, the roller-coaster-like *Jumeirah Beach Hotel* and the fantastical Madinat Jumeirah complex. There are further attractions at the thrills-and-spills Wild Wadi water park and at Ski Dubai, the Middle East's first ski slope, while more sedentary pleasures can be found at the vast Mall of the Emirates, next to Ski Dubai, of whose snowy pistes it offers superbly surreal views. Close to the Mall of the Emirates on the far side of Sheikh Zayed Road, the industrial area of Al Quoz provides an unlikely home to a number of Dubai's leading art galleries.

THE BURJ AL ARAB

Off Jumeirah Rd, Umm Suqeim
Ⓦ burj-al-arab.com. MAP P.73, POCKET MAP K15

Rising majestically from its own man-made island just off the coast of Umm Suqeim is the peerless **Burj al Arab** ("Tower of the Arabs"). Commissioned by Dubai's ruler, Sheikh Mohammed, the aim of the Burj was simple: to serve as a global icon which would put Dubai on the international map. Money was no object. The total cost of the hotel was perhaps as much as US$2 billion, and it's been estimated that even if every room in it remains full for the next hundred years, the Burj still won't pay back its original investment.

Although not much more than a decade old, the building's instantly recognizable outline has already established itself as a global symbol of Dubai to rival the Eiffel Tower, Big Ben and the Sydney Opera House. Even the top-floor helipad has acquired celebrity status: André Agassi and Roger Federer once famously played tennis on it, while Tiger Woods used it as a makeshift driving range, punting shots into the sea.

Visiting the Burj al Arab

Non-guests are only allowed into the Burj with a prior **reservation** at one of the hotel's bars, cafés or restaurants; call Ⓣ 04 301 7600 or email Ⓔ BAArestaurants@jumeirah.com. The cheapest option is to come for a cocktail at the 27th-floor *Skyview Bar* (see p.79; minimum spend 250dh/person). Alternatively, a visit for one of the Burj's sumptuous afternoon teas (285–450dh) in either the *Skyview Bar* or at the *Sahn Eddar* atrium lounge is another possibility. If you want to go the whole hog, the Burj boasts two of the city's most spectacular (and pricey) restaurants: *Al Muntaha* and *Al Mahara* (see p.78).

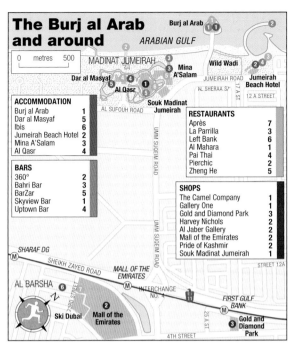

The Burj al Arab and around

| 0 metres 500 | | |

ACCOMMODATION

Burj al Arab	1
Dar al Masyaf	5
Ibis	6
Jumeirah Beach Hotel	2
Mina A'Salam	3
Al Qasr	4

BARS

360°	2
Bahri Bar	3
BarZar	5
Skyview Bar	1
Uptown Bar	4

RESTAURANTS

Après	7
La Parrilla	3
Left Bank	6
Al Mahara	1
Pai Thai	4
Pierchic	2
Zheng He	5

SHOPS

The Camel Company	1
Gallery One	1
Gold and Diamond Park	3
Harvey Nichols	2
Al Jaber Gallery	2
Mall of the Emirates	2
Pride of Kashmir	2
Souk Madinat Jumeirah	1

The Burj is home to the world's first so-called **seven-star hotel**, an expression coined by a visiting journalist to emphasize the unique levels of luxury offered within (officially, of course, such a category doesn't exist). Designed to echo the shape of a dhow's sail, the hotel's shore-facing side mainly comprises a huge sheet of white Teflon-coated fibreglass cloth, which is spectacularly illuminated by night. Most of the **interior** is actually hollow, consisting of an enormous atrium vibrantly coloured in great swathes of red, blue and green, supported by massive bulbous golden columns.

Staying here is a very expensive pleasure, and even just visiting presents certain challenges (see box opposite). Fortunately the building's magnificent exterior can be enjoyed for free from numerous vantage points nearby.

BURJ AL ARAB

JUMEIRAH BEACH HOTEL

Jumeirah Rd, Umm Suqeim. Bus #8, #88 or #X28 ⓦ bit.ly/JBHhotel. MAP P.73, POCKET MAP L15

The huge **Jumeirah Beach Hotel** (or "JBH") is the second of the area's landmark buildings, after the Burj al Arab. Designed to resemble an enormous breaking wave (although it looks more like an enormous roller coaster), and rising to a height of over 100m, the hotel was considered the most spectacular and luxurious in the city when it opened in 1997, although it has since been overtaken on both counts. It remains a fine sight, however, especially when seen from a distance in combination with the Burj al Arab, right next door, against whose slender sail it appears (with a little imagination) to be about to crash.

WILD WADI

Off Jumeirah Rd, Umm Suqeim. Bus #8, #88 or #X28 ☏ 04 348 4444, ⓦ wildwadi.com. Daily: March–May, Sept & Oct 10am–7pm; June–Aug 10am–8pm; Nov–Feb 10am–6pm. 220dh, children under 1.1m 175dh; locker and towel rental 50dh extra. MAP P.73, POCKET MAP L15

The massively popular **Wild Wadi** water park offers a variety of attractions to suit everyone from small kids to physically fit adrenaline junkies, complete with fantasy tropical lagoon, cascading waterfalls, whitewater rapids and hanging bridges. Get oriented with a circuit of the Whitewater Wadi (Master-Blaster) ride, which runs around the edge of the park, during which you're squirted on powerful jets of water up and down eleven long, twisting slides before being catapulted down the darkened Tunnel of Doom. Dedicated thrill-seekers should try the Wipeout and Riptide Flowriders, simulating powerful surfing waves, and the park's stellar attraction, the **Jumeirah Sceirah**, the tallest and fastest speed slide outside North America.

MADINAT JUMEIRAH

Al Sufouh Rd, Al Sufouh. Bus #8, #88 or #X28 ⓦ madinatjumeirah.com. MAP P.73, POCKET MAP K15–16

A vast mass of faux-Moorish-style buildings, the huge **Madinat Jumeirah** complex rises high above the coastal highway. Opened in 2005, the Madinat is one of Dubai's most spectacular modern developments: a self-contained miniature "Arabian" city comprising a vast sprawl of sand-coloured buildings topped by an extraordinary quantity of

MADINAT JUMEIRAH

wind towers, the whole thing arranged around a sequence of meandering palm-fringed waterways along which visitors are chauffeured in replica abras.

There's an undeniable whiff of Disneyland about the entire complex, admittedly, although the sheer scale of the place is strangely compelling. The Madinat also offers some of the most eye-boggling views in Dubai, with the futuristic outlines of the Burj al Arab surreally framed between medieval-looking wind towers and Moorish arcading.

The obvious place from which to explore the complex is the **Souk Madinat Jumeirah** (see p.77), though it's well worth investigating some of the superb restaurants and bars in the *Al Qasr* and *Mina A'Salam* hotels, several of which offer superlative views over the Madinat itself, the Burj al Arab and coastline.

SKI DUBAI

MALL OF THE EMIRATES

Interchange 4, Sheikh Zayed Rd. Mall of the Emirates metro ⓦ malloftheemirates.com. Daily 10am–10pm (Thurs–Sat until midnight). MAP P.73, POCKET MAP J18–K18

The second-largest mall in Dubai (outdone only by the Dubai Mall), the swanky **Mall of the Emirates** is one of the most popular in the city, packed with hundreds of shops and crowds of locals and tourists alike. Centred around a huge, glass-roofed central atrium, the mall is spread over three levels, crisscrossed by escalators and little wrought-iron bridges, and topped by the pink, five-star *Kempinski Hotel*. For dedicated shopaholics it's arguably the best place in Dubai to splash some cash (see p.76) – and there's also the added bonus of surreal views of the snow-covered slopes of Ski Dubai through huge glass walls

at the western end of the mall, or from one of the various restaurants and bars overlooking the slopes, such as *Après* (see p.77).

SKI DUBAI

Mall of the Emirates, Interchange 4, Sheikh Zayed Rd. Mall of the Emirates metro ⓣ 800-FUN, ⓦ skidxb.com. Daily: Sun–Wed 10am–11pm, Thurs 10am–midnight, Fri 9am–midnight, Sat 9am–11pm. 2hr ski slope session adult 180dh, children 150dh; ski slope day pass 300/275dh; snow park 130/120dh. MAP P.73, POCKET MAP J18

Attached to the Mall of the Emirates, the huge indoor ski resort of **Ski Dubai** is unquestionably one of the city's weirder ideas: a huge indoor snow-covered ski slope complete with regular snowfall amid the sultry heat of the Gulf. Accredited skiers and snowboarders can use five runs of varying height, steepness and difficulty, including the world's first indoor black run. There's also a Snow School ski academy for beginners and improvers, as well as a twin-track bobsled ride, a snowball-throwing gallery, snow cavern and adventure trail, plus tobogganing and snowman-building opportunities.

Shops

THE CAMEL COMPANY

Souk Madinat Jumeirah ☎ 04 368 6048,
🌐 camelcompany.ae. Daily 10am–10pm
(Thurs–Sat until midnight). MAP P.73,
POCKET MAP K16

Dubai's cutest selection of
stuffed toy camels, plus camel
mugs, camel cards, camel
T-shirts and so on. Other
branches at Dubai Mall, Souk
al Bahar, Mall of the Emirates
and Ibn Battuta Mall.

GALLERY ONE

Souk Madinat Jumeirah 🌐 g-1.com. Daily
10am–10pm (Thurs–Sat until midnight).
MAP P.73, POCKET MAP K16

Citywide chain selling a good
range of superb limited-edition
photographs of Dubai as well as
other fine-art photography and
superior postcards. Other
branches at Dubai Mall, Mall of
the Emirates, Souk Al Bahar
and JBR Walk.

GOLD AND DIAMOND PARK

Sheikh Zayed Rd between interchanges 3
and 4. First Gulf Bank metro
🌐 goldanddiamondpark.com. Daily
10am–10pm. MAP P.73, POCKET MAP L18

This low-key little mall is the
place to come if you want
diamonds, which retail here for

up to half the price you'd expect
to pay back home. You'll also
find a few other precious stones
and platinum jewellery for sale,
plus a small amount of gold.
Some places can also knock up
custom-made designs.

HARVEY NICHOLS

Mall of the Emirates. Mall of the Emirates
metro ☎ 04 409 8888, 🌐 harveynichols.com.
Daily 10am–10pm (Thurs–Sat until midnight).
MAP P.73, POCKET MAP J18

The flagship shop of one of
Dubai's flagship malls, this
suave, minimalist three-storey
department store offers a vast
array of international labels,
including British classics like
Vivienne Westwood and
Alexander McQueen.

AL JABER GALLERY

Mall of the Emirates. Mall of the Emirates
metro ☎ 04 341 4103, 🌐 aljabergallery.ae.
Daily 10am–10pm (Thurs–Sat until midnight).
MAP P.73, POCKET MAP K18

Dubai's leading purveyor of
low-grade Arabian "handi-
crafts". Look hard enough and
you might find some
half-decent stuff, including
attractive old traditional
wooden boxes and coffee pots,
though the shop is perhaps
best regarded as a source of
hilarious kitsch. Kids will love
it. Other branches at Deira
City Centre, Dubai Mall,
Souk Madinat Jumeirah and
Marina Mall.

MALL OF THE EMIRATES

Interchange 4, Sheikh Zayed Rd. Mall of the
Emirates metro 🌐 malloftheemirates.com.
Daily 10am–10pm (Thurs–Sat until midnight).
MAP P.73, POCKET MAP J18–K18

Perhaps the best one-stop
shopping destination in the city
(see p.75), with around five
hundred stores to browse, good
places to eat and drink and the
surreal snow-covered slopes of
Ski Dubai to ogle.

THE CAMEL COMPANY

PRIDE OF KASHMIR

Mall of the Emirates. Mall of the Emirates metro Ⓦ prideofkashmir.com. Daily 10am–10pm (Thurs–Sat until midnight). MAP P.73, POCKET MAP J18

One of the city's leading handicrafts chains, more upmarket than Al Jaber Gallery (see opposite) but perfectly affordable. Stock usually includes carpets and kilims alongside assorted antiques, pashminas and traditional-style wooden furniture. Other branches at Souk al Bahar and Souk Madinat Jumeirah.

SOUK MADINAT JUMEIRAH

Madinat Jumeirah Ⓦ madinatjumeirah.com. Daily 10am–10pm. MAP P.73, POCKET MAP K16

At the heart of the Madinat Jumeirah, this superb re-creation of a "traditional" souk serves up a beguiling mix of shopping, eating and drinking opportunities. Like all good bazaars, the layout is mazy and disorienting, although you'll never be far from where you want to be. Shops include branches of Al Jaber Gallery, Pride of Kashmir, The Camel Company and Gallery One (see opposite).

Restaurants

APRÈS

Mall of the Emirates. Mall of the Emirates metro Ⓣ 04 341 2575. Daily 11.30am–1am (Thurs & Fri until 2am). MAP P.73, POCKET MAP J18

Cool bar-restaurant with surreal views over the snowy slopes of Ski Dubai through big picture windows and a good range of international food (mains 85–160dh) – anything from bouillabaisse to fish and chips, plus excellent thin-crust pizzas (around 70dh). It's also a fun spot for a drink, with an extensive drinks selection and kick-ass cocktails.

SOUK MADINAT JUMEIRAH

LA PARRILLA

25th floor, Jumeirah Beach Hotel, Jumeirah Rd Ⓣ 04 406 8999, Ⓦ bit.ly/JBHhotel. Daily 6.30pm–midnight. MAP P.73, POCKET MAP L15

Perched atop the *Jumeirah Beach Hotel*, this Argentinian-themed steakhouse boasts superb views of the Burj al Arab, excellent Argentinian, Australian and Wagyu steaks (165–475dh) and an appealing splash of Latin atmosphere, with live music and tango dancers nightly (except Sunday) – ask nicely and the manageress might even sing you a song.

LEFT BANK

Souk Madinat Jumeirah Ⓣ 04 368 6171. Daily 10.30am–2am (Wed–Fri until 3am). MAP P.73, POCKET MAP K16

Jostling for elbow room among the string of incredibly popular places along the Souk Madinat Jumeirah waterfront, this sleek modern bar-restaurant is a good vantage point if you can bag a table on the outside terrace. The regularly changing menu (mains 90–165dh) features an eclectic selection of good (if pricey) international food – wild sea bass or confit duck leg through to curry of the day or Lancashire hotpot. Or just come for a drink.

AL MAHARA

Burj al Arab ☎ 04 301 7600, ⓦ burj-al-arab
.com. Daily 12.30–3pm & 7pm–midnight.
MAP P.73, POCKET MAP K15

Perhaps the more appealing of
the Burj al Arab's two signature
restaurants, *Al Mahara* looks
like some kind of fantastic
underwater grotto, entered
through a huge golden arch and
with seats arranged around a
giant fish tank. There's a range of
gourmet international seafood
to choose from plus a couple
of meat options, although the
prices are enough to make you
weep into your obsiblue
shrimps. Mains around 370dh.

PAI THAI

Al Qasr Hotel, Madinat Jumeirah ☎ 04 366
8888. Daily 6–11.30pm. MAP P.73, POCKET MAP K15
This beautiful Thai restaurant is
one of the city's most romantic
places to eat, with stunning
Burj al Arab views from the
candlelit terrace and live music
murmuring gently in the
background. Food includes all
the usual Thai classics, such as
spicy salads, meat and seafood
curries – not the most original
menu in town, although given
the setting you probably won't
care. Mains 80–200dh.

PIERCHIC

Al Qasr Hotel, Madinat Jumeirah ☎ 04 366
8888. Daily 1–3pm & 7–11.30pm. MAP P.73,
POCKET MAP K15

One of the city's most spectacularly situated restaurants,
perched at the end of a breezy
pier jutting out in front of the
grandiose *Al Qasr* hotel, and
with unbeatable views of the
nearby Burj al Arab, *Jumeirah
Beach Hotel* and Madinat
Jumeirah. The short, mainly
seafood menu has prices to
match the location, with a
selection of international-style
fine-dining fish and seafood
offerings, ranging from Dover
sole to Canadian lobster, plus a
couple of meat choices. Mains
around 200dh.

ZHENG HE

Mina A'Salam Hotel, Madinat Jumeirah
☎ 04 366 6730. Daily noon–3pm &
7–11.30pm. MAP P.73, POCKET MAP K15
Classy Chinese restaurant
dishing up top-notch fine
dining. There's nothing
particularly innovative about
the menu (mains 90–180dh),
although quality is high and
the setting memorable, with
seating either inside the svelte
restaurant or outside on the
beautiful Burj-facing terrace.

Bars

360°

Jumeirah Beach Hotel, Jumeirah Rd ☎ 04
406 8769, ⓦ 360dubai.com. Daily 5pm–2am.
MAP P.73, POCKET MAP L15
The ultimate Dubaian chill-out
bar (if you don't mind the high
prices and sometimes erratic
service), spectacularly located
at the end of a long breakwater
which arcs out into the Gulf
opposite the *Jumeirah Beach
Hotel* and Burj al Arab, and
offering sublime after-dark
views of both. Occasionally

there's an entrance charge when visiting DJs are in residence; you may also need to reserve in advance if planning to arrive before 10pm – check the website for details.

BAHRI BAR

Mina A'Salam, Madinat Jumeirah ☎ 04 366 6730; Daily 4pm–2am (Thurs & Fri until 3am). MAP P.73, POCKET MAP K15

Superb little Arabian-style outdoor terrace, liberally scattered with canopied sofas, Moorish artefacts and Persian carpets, and offering drop-dead gorgeous views of the Burj and Madinat Jumeirah – particularly gorgeous towards sunset.

BARZAR

Souk Madinat Jumeirah ☎ 04 366 6730. Daily 5pm–2am (Tues, Thurs & Fri until 3am). MAP P.73, POCKET MAP K16

The bar here is pretty nondescript, but the big terrace outside is one of the Madinat's best chill-out spaces, with views of the fake Arabian wind towers and waterways and lots of bean-bags to crash out on over drinks, plus a good range of shisha.

SKYVIEW BAR

Burj al Arab ☎ 04 301 7600. ✉ BAArestaurants@jumeirah.com. Daily: afternoon tea 1–6pm; drinks 7pm–2am. MAP P.73, POCKET MAP K15

Landmark bar perched near the summit of the Burj al Arab, with colourful psychedelic decor and vast sea and city views – coming for a drink here is currently the cheapest way to see the inside of this fabulous hotel. The huge drinks list majors in cocktails (from 100dh), but also sports a decent spread of wines, spirits, mocktails and even a few beers; alternatively, go for the lavish, seven-course afternoon teas (450dh). There's a minimum spend of 250dh per person, and you'll need to reserve in advance via email.

UPTOWN BAR

Jumeirah Beach Hotel, Jumeirah Rd ☎ 04 406 8769. ⓦ bit.ly/JBHhotel. Daily 6pm–1.30am. MAP P.73, POCKET MAP L15

Superb views of the Burj al Arab and southern Dubai are the main draw at this place, located on the 24th floor of the *Jumeirah Beach Hotel*. There's indoor and outdoor seating, plus a reasonable drinks list, although the decor is disappointingly humdrum for such a fine location.

Pacha comes to Dubai

Dubai looks set to get its first international **superclub** in early 2014 with the arrival of global über-brand Pacha, hot from its Ibizan homeland. Occupying a prime location in Souk Madinat Jumeirah, **Pacha Dubai** will host regular big-name visiting DJs who will command a huge new floor space carved out of the area formerly occupied by the long-running venues *Trilogy* and *Jambase*. Check *Time Out Dubai* for latest details.

The Palm Jumeirah and Dubai Marina

Nowhere is the scale of Dubai's explosive growth as staggeringly obvious as in the far south of the city, home to the vast Palm Jumeirah artificial island and Dubai Marina development – evidence of the emirate's magical ability to turn sand into skyscrapers and raise entire new city suburbs up out of the waves. In the early 2000s this whole area was more or less desert. Then the developers moved in. By mid-decade the district had turned into the largest construction site on the planet. Ten years on and the cranes and building crews have gone, leaving a brand-new city and the world's largest man-made island in their wake, with a forest of densely packed skyscrapers lined up around the glitzy marina itself and the fronds of the Palm spreading out into the waters beyond.

THE PALM JUMEIRAH

Monorail trains 2–3 hourly; 15dh one way. 25dh return. POCKET MAP D10–G15

Lying off the coast around 5km south of the Burj al Arab and stretching 4km out into the waters of the Arabian Gulf, **The Palm Jumeirah** – the biggest artificial island in the world – has doubled the length of the Dubai coastline at a total cost of over US$12 billion. As its name

suggests, the Palm Jumeirah is designed in the shape of a palm tree, with a central "trunk" and a series of sixteen radiating "fronds", the whole enclosed in an 11km-long breakwater, or "crescent", lined with a string of huge, upmarket resorts.

The best way to see the Palm is from the **Palm Jumeirah Monorail**, whose driverless trains shuttle along an elevated track between the *Atlantis*

Dubai's artificial islands

For a city with aspirations of taking over the world's tourism industry, Dubai has a serious lack of one thing: **coast**. In its natural state, the emirate boasts a mere 70km of shoreline, totally insufficient for its various needs. Dubai's solution to its pressing lack of waterfront was characteristically bold: it decided to build some more. The Palm Jumeirah was just the first (and smallest) of four proposed offshore developments. Two further palm-shaped islands – the **Palm Jebel Ali**, 20km further down the coast, and the gargantuan **Palm Deira**, right next to the old city centre – were also planned, although work on both has been on hold for several years. The current status of the even more fanciful **The World** development is similarly uncertain. Lying around 5km off the coast, this complex of artificial islands has been constructed in the shape of an approximate map of the world. Although physical reclamation of the islands has been complete since around 2006, most of the islands remain uninhabited dots of sand in the ocean.

resort and the mainland, offering sweeping views over the Palm, although unfortunately the monorail doesn't connect with the Dubai metro or anywhere else useful.

ATLANTIS

Crescent Rd, Palm Jumeirah ☏ 04 426 0000, ⓦ atlantisthepalm.com. Monorail trains 2–3 hourly; 15dh one way, 25dh return. Aquaventure 225dh, or 180dh for children under 1.2m. Dolphin Bay 800–900dh; includes admission to Aquaventure. The Lost Chambers daily 10am–11pm; 100dh; children aged 3–11 70dh; under 2s free. POCKET MAP E10–F10

At the furthest end of the Palm Jumeirah, the vast **Atlantis** resort is the island's major landmark: an outlandish pink colossus perched over the sea like some kind of weird triumphal arch. What it lacks in architectural taste, it does at least partly make up for in on-site facilities and (pricey) activities. Best is the spectacular **Aquaventure** waterpark, featuring an adrenaline-charged array of rides and slides centred on the dramatic "Ziggurat", where you'll find the park's headline Leap of Faith waterslide – 27.5m tall, it catapults you at stomach-

churning speed down into a transparent tunnel amid a lagoon full of sharks. There are further watery attractions at **Dolphin Bay**, next door, which offers visitors the chance to swim with the hotel's troupe of resident bottlenose dolphins.

Alternatively, head to **The Lost Chambers**, a sequence of halls and tunnels running through the hotel's vast underground aquarium, populated by an extraordinary array of 65,000-odd tropical fish and dotted with assorted Atlantis-style "ruins".

THE LOST CHAMBERS, ATLANTIS

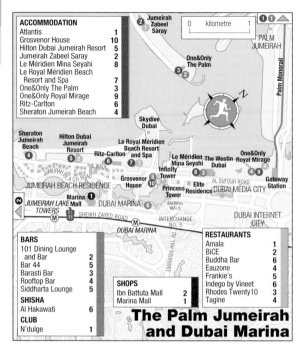

ACCOMMODATION
Atlantis	1
Grosvenor House	10
Hilton Dubai Jumeirah Resort	5
Jumeirah Zabeel Saray	2
Le Méridien Mina Seyahi	8
Le Royal Méridien Beach Resort and Spa	7
One&Only The Palm	3
One&Only Royal Mirage	9
Ritz-Carlton	6
Sheraton Jumeirah Beach	4

BARS
101 Dining Lounge and Bar	2
Bar 44	5
Barasti Bar	3
Rooftop Bar	4
Siddharta Lounge	5

SHISHA
Al Hakawati	6

CLUB
N'dulge	1

SHOPS
Ibn Battuta Mall	2
Marina Mall	1

RESTAURANTS
Amala	1
BiCE	2
Buddha Bar	6
Eauzone	4
Frankie's	5
Indego by Vineet	6
Rhodes Twenty10	3
Tagine	4

The Palm Jumeirah and Dubai Marina

DUBAI MARINA

Dubai Marina or Jumeirah Lake Towers metros. MAP P.82, POCKET MAP A15–D16

A vast phalanx of tightly packed high-rises signals the appearance of **Dubai Marina**, Dubai's brand-new city-within-a-city, built at lightning speed since 2005. Like much of modern Dubai, the marina is a mishmash of the good, the bad and the downright ugly. Many of the high-rises are of minimal architectural distinction, and all are packed so closely together that the overall effect is of hyperactive urban development gone completely mad. The whole area feels oddly piecemeal and under-planned, while the lack of pedestrian facilities (excepting the pleasant oceanfront promenade and Marina Walk; see p.84) means that you're unlikely to see much

more of it than can be glimpsed while speeding down Sheikh Zayed Road by car or metro.

It's weirdly impressive, even so, especially by night, when darkness hides the worst examples of gimcrack design and the whole area lights up into a fabulous display of airy neon (or, if you prefer, a display of high-rise ecological catastrophe waiting to happen).

DUBAI INTERNET AND MEDIA CITIES

Nakheel metro. MAP P.82, POCKET MAP D16–E16

At the north end of Dubai Marina lie **Dubai Internet City** and **Dubai Media City** – the first and most successful in a string of dedicated business areas set up by the government to lure foreign firms to the city under preferential commercial terms. There's not much really to see here, though travelling

DUBAI MARINA BEACH

up and down Sheikh Zayed Road or on the metro you can't fail to notice the soaring **Al Kazim Towers** – a pair of quirky skyscrapers styled after New York's iconic Chrysler Building.

JUMEIRAH BEACH RESIDENCE AND THE WALK

Dubai Marina metro. Covent Garden Market ⓦ coventgardenmarket.ae; Wed & Thurs 5pm–midnight, Fri & Sat 10am–9pm. MAP P.82, POCKET MAP A15–B15

Most of Dubai Marina's tourist development is focused on the string of luxurious **beachside hotels** which established themselves here when the coast was largely undeveloped, but now find themselves tragically hemmed in by densely packed high-rises on all sides. Notable among these is the unlovely **Jumeirah Beach Residence** (JBR): a 1.7km-long sprawl of forty high-rises with living space for ten thousand people. The JBR's one redeeming feature is **The Walk**, an attractive promenade lined with boutiques, pizzerias, coffee shops, burger joints and fast-food outlets – one of the very few places in the new city which positively encourages people to get out of their cars. It also boasts a modicum of street life including, during winter months, the pleasant **Covent Garden Market**, with stalls selling clothes, jewellery and other collectibles.

Marina beaches

All Dubai's **beach hotels** allow non-guests to use their beaches, swimming pools and other facilities for a (usually hefty) fee, although some places close to outsiders when occupancy levels rise above a certain percentage. Rates vary from around 100dh per day midweek at the *Sheraton Jumeirah Beach* up to 500dh at the *Ritz-Carlton*. Given the wallet-emptying amounts of money involved, many people prefer to head to the stretch of **free beach** between the *Sheraton* and *Hilton* hotels, which has plenty of white sand to loll about on, though there are several other free or cheap beaches. All the marina beach hotels have **watersports centres**, offering a wide range of activities including windsurfing, sailing, kayaking, waterskiing, wake-boarding and parasailing (but not jet-skiing, which the authorities have banned).

Dubai: the world's tallest city

D ubai is now officially the tallest city on the planet: at the time of writing it was home to 23 of the world's 100 highest buildings. By comparison, traditional high-rise hotspots Hong Kong and Chicago muster just seven top-100 buildings apiece, while New York and Shanghai manage just four – the same as Abu Dhabi. The landmark example of Dubai's sky-high ambition is provided by the staggering Burj Khalifa (see p.61), while other high-rise icons include the Burj al Arab (see p.72) and the glittering Emirates Towers (see p.58), as well as less well-known buildings such as the twin towers of the recently opened *JW Marriott Marquis Dubai* (see p.62), the world's tallest hotel.

MARINA WALK

Marina or Jumeirah Lake Towers metros.
MAP P.82, POCKET MAP B16–C16

Dubai's **marina** is actually a man-made sea inlet, lined with luxury yachts and fancy speedboats, which snakes inland behind the JBR, running parallel with the coast for around 1.5km. Encircling the water is the attractive pedestrianized promenade known as **Marina Walk**, its long straggle of waterfront cafés and restaurants enjoyably lively after dark. Presiding over the northern sea inlet into the marina is the quirky **Infinity Tower** (330m), the latest in

Dubai's increasingly long list of iconic skyscrapers and instantly recognizable thanks to its distinctively twisted outline, which rotates through 90 degrees from base to summit – a bit like the famous Turning Tower in Malmö, Sweden.

Various kiosks around Marina Walk offer a mix of expensive **boat** charters alongside much cheaper dhow cruises for those who want to take to the water.

IBN BATTUTA MALL

Between interchanges 5 and 6 (exits 25 and 27), Sheikh Zayed Rd. Ibn Battuta metro
🌐 ibnbattutamall.com. Daily 10am–10pm (Thurs–Sat until midnight). POCKET MAP A16

The outlandish, mile-long **Ibn Battuta Mall** is undoubtedly Dubai's wackiest shopping experience. The mall is themed in six different sections after some of the places – Morocco, Andalucia, Tunisia, Persia, India and China – visited by the famous Arab traveller Ibn Battuta. Highlights include a life-size elephant complete with mechanical mahout (rider), a twilit Tunisian village and a full-size Chinese junk, while the lavishness of some of the decoration would seem more appropriate on a Rajput palace or a Persian grand mosque than a motorway mall.

MARINA WALK, DUBAI MARINA

Shops

IBN BATTUTA MALL

Between interchanges 5 and 6, Sheikh Zayed Rd. Ibn Battuta metro Ⓦibnbattutamall.com. Daily 10am–10pm (Thurs–Sat until midnight). POCKET MAP A16

This Ibn Battuta-inspired mall is worth a visit for its stunning decor alone (see opposite) – although as a shopping experience it's a bit underpowered. Shops include a handy Borders bookstore, a well-stocked branch of the local Toy Store chain and the chic Ginger & Lace ladieswear boutique – and it's worth a look at the entertaining Daiso in the Andalucia court, a kind of Japanese pound shop with everything for 7dh.

MARINA MALL

Sheikh Zayed Rd. Jumeirah Lake Towers metro Ⓦmarinamall.ae. Daily 10am–10pm (Thurs & Fri until midnight). MAP P.82, POCKET MAP B16

Aimed more at local marina residents than visiting tourists, this bright modern mall is worth a visit if you're in the area and fancy a bit of clothes shopping (the central atrium looks like a kind of

postmodern temple of designer brands), but not worth a special visit otherwise.

Restaurants

AMALA

Jumeirah Zabeel Saray hotel, Palm Jumeirah Ⓣ04 453 0444, Ⓦjumeirah.com. Daily 6pm–1am. MAP P.82, POCKET MAP C13

The most popular of the *Zabeel Saray*'s stunning collection of restaurants, as opulently decorated as a Bollywood film set and with decent North Indian cooking. The fixed price of 285dh per head allows you to order as much as you like from the à la carte menu – good value, assuming you arrive sufficiently hungry.

BICE

Hilton Jumeirah Beach Resort, Dubai Marina. Jumeirah Lake Towers metro Ⓣ04 318 2520, Ⓦhilton.com. Daily 12.30–3pm & 7–11.30pm. MAP P.82, POCKET MAP B15

Polished modern Italian – reckoned by some to be best in the southern city – serving up tasty pizzas and pastas (70–90dh) bursting with fresh ingredients and flavours, plus a mix of more elaborate meat and seafood mains (from 170dh).

BUDDHA BAR

Grosvenor House Hotel, Dubai Marina. Dubai Marina metro Ⓣ04 317 6833, Ⓦbuddhabar.com. Daily 8pm–2am (Thurs & Fri until 3am). MAP P.82, POCKET MAP C16

Modelled after the famous Parisian joint, this superb bar-restaurant is a sight in its own right: a huge, sepulchral space hung with dozens of red-lantern chandeliers. The menu features a fine array of Japanese and pan-Asian cooking – pricey (mains around 200dh), but worth it for the ambience. Advance reservations recommended.

IBN BATTUTA MALL

EAUZONE

Arabian Courtyard, One&Only Royal Mirage, Dubai Marina. Nakheel metro ☎ 04 315 2412, ⓦ royalmirage.oneandonlyresorts.com. Daily noon–11.30pm. MAP P.82, POCKET MAP E15

Regularly voted Dubai's most romantic restaurant with seating amid the beautifully floodlit waters of one of the hotel's swimming pools. The obligatory evening set menus (from 260dh) feature European meat and seafood dishes, some with an Asian twist. Reserve ahead.

FRANKIE'S

The Walk at Jumeirah Beach Residence, Dubai Marina. Dubai Marina metro ☎ 04 399 4311, ⓦ facebook.com/FrankiesDubai. Daily 6.30pm–12.30am. MAP P.82, POCKET MAP B15

The foodie lovechild of champion jockey Frankie Dettori in association with Marco Pierre White, this cosy restaurant has a casual bistro feel, with hints of American family diner and a mixed Italian menu of reasonably priced pizzas and pastas (from 70dh), plus fancier meat and seafood mains (from 150dh).

INDEGO BY VINEET

Grosvenor House Hotel, Dubai Marina. Dubai Marina metro ☎ 04 317 6000, ⓦ luxurycollection.com/grosvenorhouse. Daily 12.30–3pm (Fri & Sat until 4pm) & 7pm–midnight. MAP P.82, POCKET MAP C15

Overseen by Vineet Bhatia, India's first Michelin-starred chef, this stylish restaurant showcases his contemporary Indian cooking, blending subcontinental and international ingredients and techniques to unusual effect. Mains 140–220dh.

RHODES TWENTY10

Le Royal Méridien, Dubai Marina. Dubai Marina metro ☎ 04 316 5505, ⓦ leroyalmeridien-dubai.com. Daily except Mon 7pm–midnight. MAP P.82, POCKET MAP C15

Casual and affordable, Gary Rhodes' second Dubai restaurant features an excellent range of "European-inspired cuisine infused with a touch of the Middle East" alongside burgers, steaks and British classics like steak-and-kidney pie. Most mains 120–190dh.

TAGINE

The Palace, One&Only Royal Mirage, Dubai Marina. Nakheel metro ☎ 04 315 2412, ⓦ royalmirage.oneandonlyresorts.com. Daily except Mon 7–11.30pm (last orders). MAP P.82, POCKET MAP E15

Sumptuous little Moroccan restaurant, the beautiful Moorish decor complemented by authentic North African cooking including classics like *pastilla* (pigeon pie), *tangia* and a selection of delicious tagines. Mains around 100dh.

Bars

101 DINING LOUNGE AND BAR

One&Only The Palm, Palm Jumeirah ☎ 04 440 1030, ⓦ thepalm.oneandonlyresorts.com. Daily 11am–1am. MAP P.82, POCKET MAP C14

Overlooking the swish new *One&Only The Palm*'s private marina, *101*'s big draws are its gorgeous terrace over the water outside (live DJ most evenings) and stunning views across to the marina's skyscrapers opposite.

EAUZONE

BAR 44

44th floor, Grosvenor House Hotel, Dubai Marina. Dubai Marina metro ☎ 04 399 8888, ⓦ luxurycollection.com/grosvenorhouse. Daily 6pm–2am (Thurs until 3am). MAP P.82, POCKET MAP C15

This svelte contemporary bar offers peerless 360-degree views of the entire marina development, with twinkling high-rises stretching away in every direction and a big selection of wallet-emptying champagnes, cool cocktails and other designer beverages.

BARASTI BAR

Le Méridien Mina Sehayi, Dubai Marina. Nakheel metro ☎ 04 318 1313, ⓦ barastibeach .com. Daily noon–2am. MAP P.82, POCKET MAP D15

Fun, two-level beachside bar popular with an eclectic crowd. Downstairs is usually more Ibiza chill-out, with ambient music, shisha and loungers on the sand; the pubbier upstairs is generally noisier, with live DJs and a party atmosphere.

ROOFTOP BAR

Arabian Court, One&Only Royal Mirage, Dubai Marina. Nakheel metro ☎ 04 315 2412, ⓦ royalmirage.oneandonlyresorts.com. Daily 5pm–1am. MAP P.82, POCKET MAP E15

One of Dubai's ultimate Orientalist fantasies, with seductive Moorish decor, cushion-strewn pavilions, silver-tray tables and other assorted Arabiah artefacts. A smooth live DJ adds to the *One Thousand and One Nights* ambience.

SIDDHARTA LOUNGE

Tower Two, Grosvenor House Hotel. Dubai Marina metro ☎ 04 317 6000, ⓦ luxurycollection.com/grosvenorhouse. Daily 5pm–1am, Thurs and Fri until 2am. MAP P.82, POCKET MAP C16

Swanky new venue with a cool poolside terrace and bar outside and a "palm area" with shisha lounge within – all snowy-white decor with the occasional gold

ROOFTOP BAR

armchair. Food and drinks are ordered off the menu of the adjacent *Buddha Bar* (see p.85).

Shisha

AL HAKAWATI

Marina Walk, Dubai Marina. Dubai Marina metro ☎ 04 368 2346, ⓦ alhakawaticafe.com. Daily 9am–2am. MAP P.82, POCKET MAP C16

Though the sign's easy to miss, this lively café is pretty obvious, with an eye-catching scatter of red, kilim-covered sofas shaded by a little grove of potted trees. There are ten types of shisha on offer (21dh), and the food – a mishmash of Arabian and Western – isn't bad either.

Club

N'DULGE

Atlantis resort, Palm Jumeirah ☎ 04 426 0561, ⓦ atlantisthepalm.com. Daily 9pm–3am. POCKET MAP E10

Dubai's leading super-club, with space for around 3000 punters on its two big dancefloors inside and a lovely chill-out and shisha terrace outside. The eclectic music policy, with different tunes in each of the three areas, means you should find something you like.

Sharjah

Just 10km north up the coast, the city of Sharjah seems at first sight like simply an extension of Dubai, with whose northern suburbs it now merges seamlessly in an ugly concrete sprawl. Physically, the two cities may have virtually fused into one, but culturally they remain light years apart. Sharjah has a distinctively different flavour, having clung much more firmly to its traditional Islamic roots, exemplified by a fine array of museums devoted to various aspects of Islamic culture and local Emirati life. These include the world-class Museum of Islamic Civilization, the excellent Sharjah Art Gallery, the impressive new Sharjah Heritage Museum, and the engaging Al Mahatta aviation museum. Other attractions include the massive Blue Souk, one of the largest in the UAE, and Souq al Arsa, one of the prettiest.

SHARJAH MUSEUM OF ISLAMIC CIVILIZATION

Corniche St ☎ 06 565 5455, ⓦ islamicmuseum.ae. Sat–Thurs 8am–8pm, Fri 4–8pm. 5dh. MAP P.89

The main reason for trekking out to Sharjah is to visit the superb **Sharjah Museum of Islamic Civilization**, which occupies the beautifully restored waterfront Souk al

SHARJAH MUSEUM OF ISLAMIC CIVILIZATION

Majara building, topped with a distinctive golden dome. The museum is spread over two levels. Downstairs, the **Abu Bakr Gallery of Islamic Faith** has extensive displays on the elaborate rituals associated with the traditional Haj pilgrimage to Mecca, while the **Ibn al Haitham Gallery of Science and Technology** showcases the extensive contributions made by Arab scholars to scientific innovation over the centuries. The first floor of the museum is devoted to four galleries offering a chronological overview of **Islamic arts and crafts**, with superb displays of historic manuscripts, ceramics, glass, armour, woodwork, textiles and jewellery. Exhibits include the first-ever map of the then known world (ie Eurasia), created by Moroccan cartographer Al Shereef al Idrisi in 1099 – a surprisingly accurate document, although slightly baffling at first sight since it's oriented upside down, with south at the top.

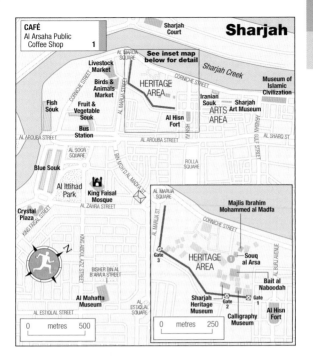

CAFÉ
Al Arsaha Public Coffee Shop 1

Sharjah Court

Sharjah

See inset map below for detail

AL MARIJA SQUARE

Sharjah Creek

Museum of Islamic Civilization

Livestock Market

CORNICHE STREET

Birds & Animals Market

HERITAGE AREA

CORNICHE STREET

Iranian Souk

Sharjah Art Museum

ARTS AREA

Fish Souk

Fruit & Vegetable Souk

Al Hisn Fort

CORNICHE STREET

AL MARIJA STREET

Bus Station

AL AROUBA STREET

AL AROUBA STREET

AL SHARQ STREET

ARABIAN GULF STREET

AL SOOR SQUARE

ROLLA SQUARE

Blue Souk

Al Ittihad Park

King Faisal Mosque

IBN MOHD AL MADFA ST

AL ZAHRA STREET

AL MARIJA SQUARE

Majlis Ibrahim Mohammed al Madfa

CORNICHE STREET

Crystal Plaza

KING FAISAL STREET

KING ABDUL AZIZ STREET

AL MARIJA ST

Gate 3

HERITAGE AREA

Souq al Arsa

AL BURJ AVENUE

BISHER BIN AL B'ARA'A STREET

Bait al Naboodah

Al Mahatta Museum

AL ESTIQLAL STREET

AL ESTIQLAL SQUARE

Sharjah Heritage Museum

Gate 2

Gate 1

Al Hisn Fort

Calligraphy Museum

0 metres 500

0 metres 250

SHARJAH CREEK

MAP P.89

Sharjah's broad **Creek** describes a leisurely parabola around the northern edge of the city centre before terminating in the expansive Khaled Lagoon. Despite being long since eclipsed by Dubai's various ports, Sharjah's Creek still sees a considerable amount of commercial shipping both modern and traditional, usually with a few old-fashioned wooden dhows moored up on the far side of the water beneath a long line of spiky gantries.

SHARJAH ART MUSEUM

Just off Corniche St; from the waterfront follow the sign to the Corniche Post Office and then to the Sharjah Art Foundation, or access from Al Burj Ave, behind Al Hisn fort ☎ 06 568 8222, ✪ sharjahmuseums.ae. Sat–Thurs 8am–8pm, Fri 4–8pm. Free. MAP P.89

Occupying a large modern wind-towered building, the **Sharjah Art Museum** is the major showpiece in Sharjah's attempts to position itself as a serious player in the international art scene. Temporary exhibitions of varying quality feature on the ground floor. Much more interesting is the permanent **Orientalist collection** upstairs, which focuses on paintings by nineteenth-century European artists depicting life in Islamic lands. Highlight is a wonderful selection of lithographs by Scottish artist David Roberts drawn from his celebrated *Sketches in the Holy Land and Syria*: a quintessential visual expression of Orientalism, with canvases showing picturesquely robed natives reclining among picturesque mosques, forts and assorted ruins.

89

AL HISN FORT

Al Burj Ave. MAP P.89

At the heart of the city is the modest **Al Hisn Fort** of 1820, the most enduring symbol of old Sharjah, formerly home to the ruling Al Qassimi family, although it's now ignominiously hemmed in by ugly apartment blocks. The fort is currently closed for extensive renovations, with no reopening date in sight.

HERITAGE AREA

MAP P.89

The area west of Al Hisn Fort was formerly the heart of old Sharjah, an old-fashioned quarter of traditional Emirati houses arranged around a sequence of spacious, lopsided squares and labyrinthine alleyways, and enclosed in a long section of reconstructed city wall. The entire area has now been meticulously renovated and relaunched as the city's so-called **Heritage Area**, home to several interesting museums and the Souq al Arsa.

SOUQ AL ARSA AND AROUND

Heritage Area. Most shops open 10am–1/2pm & 4/5–10pm (closed Fri morning). MAP P.89

The **Souq al Arsa**, which bounds the northern side of the Heritage Area, is far and away

the prettiest in Sharjah. The souk is centred around an atmospheric central pillared courtyard, flanked by the personable little *Al Arsaha Public Coffee Shop* (see opposite), beyond which radiates an intriguing tangle of alleyways. The coral-stone shops are stuffed full of all sorts of colourful local handicrafts as well as an eclectic selection of curios and collectibles.

Tucked away around the back (north) side of the Souq al Arsa is the attractive **Majlis Ibrahim Mohammed al Madfa**, topped by a diminutive round wind tower, said to be the only one in the UAE.

BAIT AL NABOODAH

Opposite the Souq al Arsa, Heritage Area ☎ 06 568 1738, ⍾ sharjahmuseums.ae. Sat–Thurs 8am–8pm, Fri 4–8pm. 5dh. MAP P.89

Situated in an atmospheric old house, the **Bait al Naboodah** offers an interesting re-creation of traditional family life in Sharjah. The main draw is the rambling two-storey building itself, one of the most attractive in the UAE, arranged around a spacious central courtyard. Only the rooms on the ground floor are open, including a string of bedrooms furnished in traditional Gulf

CANNON AT AL HISN FORT

style, with canopied wooden beds and floor cushions, the walls hung with old rifles, clocks and radios.

SHARJAH HERITAGE MUSEUM

Heritage Area ☎ 06 568 0006. ⓦ sharjahmuseums.ae. Sat–Thurs 8am–8pm, Fri 4–8pm. Free. MAP P.89

The excellent new **Sharjah Heritage Museum** is one of the best collections of its kind anywhere in the UAE. Wide-ranging and well-explained exhibits cover all the usual bases – traditional dress, architecture, social customs, the pearling trade and so on – with many insights into lesser-known local customs en route.

THE BLUE SOUK

King Faisal St, 1km west of the city centre (about 6dh by taxi). Most shops open roughly 10am–10pm, although many close around 1–4pm. MAP P.89

The huge **Blue Souk** (officially known as the Central Souk) occupies an enormous, eye-catching and ungainly pair of buildings topped by myriad wind towers and clad in brilliant blue tiling. The souk is best known for its numerous carpet shops, which stock a vast range of Persian and other rugs (usually) at significantly lower prices than in Dubai.

AL MAHATTA MUSEUM

Bisher bin al Bara'a St (Street 23), off King Abdul Aziz St (around 9dh by taxi from the centre) ☎ 06 573 3079, ⓦ bit.ly/AlMahatta. Sat–Thurs 8am–8pm, Fri 4–8pm. 5dh. MAP P.89

Devoted to the history of aviation in Sharjah, the **Al Mahatta Museum** is unexpectedly absorbing. It occupies the buildings of what was until 1977 the city's airport, complete with aircraft hangar and air traffic control tower (the runway was incorporated into what is now King Abdul Aziz Street). The

THE BLUE SOUK

cavernous **hangar** contains five antique planes (plus the nose of a 1952 De Havilland Comet, the world's first commercial jet aircraft) dating from the 1930s to the 1950s, while the remainder of the museum occupies the old airport **rest house**, with fascinating displays about the first commercial flights to Sharjah (launched in 1932 by Imperial Airways) and other exhibits.

Café

AL ARSAHA PUBLIC COFFEE SHOP

Souq al Arsa. Daily 8am–9pm. MAP P.89

This quaint little café offers a beguiling window on local life, with old photos of the UAE on the rattan-covered walls, colourful tables covered in big Lipton's tea logos and an entertaining local clientele. It's a good place for a glass of mint tea or a cup of coffee, and they also serve up mountainous, spicy biriyanis (chicken, mutton or fish; 20dh).

Al Ain

For a complete change of pace and scenery, a day-trip out to the sedate desert city of Al Ain, some 130km inland (a two-hour minibus ride) from Dubai on the border with Oman, offers the perfect antidote to the rip-roaring pace of life on the coast. The UAE's fourth-largest city and only major inland settlement, Al Ain – and the twin city of Buraimi, on the Omani side of the border – grew up around the string of six oases whose densely packed swathes of palms still dot the modern city. The city served as an important staging post on trading routes between Oman and the Gulf, a fact attested to by the numerous forts that dot the area and by the rich archeological remains found in the vicinity, evidence of continuous settlement dating back to Neolithic times.

AL AIN NATIONAL MUSEUM AND AROUND

Off Zayed bin Sultan St ☎ 03 764 1595, ⓦ bit.ly/AlAinMuseum. Sat, Sun & Tues–Thurs 8.30am–7.30pm, Fri 3–7.30pm, closed Mon. 3dh. MAP P.93

The old-fashioned **Al Ain National Museum** is well worth a look before diving into the rest of the city. The first section sports the usual dusty displays on local life and culture, while the second offers a comprehensive overview of the archeology of the UAE.

Right next to the museum, the **Sultan bin Zayed Fort** (or Eastern Fort) is one of the eighteen or so scattered around Al Ain. The picturesque three-towered structure is best known as the birthplace of Sheikh Zayed bin Sultan al Nahyan (ruled 1966–2004), who oversaw the transformation of the emirate from impoverished Arabian backwater into today's oil-rich contemporary city-state.

AL AIN OASIS

Between Al Ain St and Zayed bin Sultan St, south of the centre. Daily sunrise–sunset. Free. MAP P.93

A dusty green wall of palms announces the beautiful **Al Ain Oasis**, with a mazy network of little walled lanes running between the densely planted thickets of trees including an estimated 150,000-odd date palms. There are eight entrances dotted around the perimeter of the oasis, although given the disorienting tangle of roads within you're unlikely to end up coming out where you entered.

KHANJAR (DAGGER), AL AIN NATIONAL MUSEUM

Map labels

Hili Gardens and Archeological Park (5km) & **1** (35km)

Fruit & Vegetable Souk

Al Ain

Al Khandaq Fort

BURAIMI

ACCOMMODATION
Al Maha Desert Resort and Spa   1

CAFÉ AND RESTAURANT
Al Diwan   2
The Hut   1

OMAN
U.A.E.

MOHAMMED BIN KHALFA ST

131ST STREET

BURAIMI SHAKHBOOT BIN SULTAN STREET

OMAR BIN AL KHATTAB STREET

ALI BIN ABI TALEB ST GLOBE R/A

ABU BAKR AL SIDDIQ ST

KHALIFA BIN ZAYED STREET

AL AIN

118TH ST

ZAYED BIN SULTAN STREET

CLOCK TOWER R/A

Al Muraba'a Fort

OTHMAN BIN AFFAN STREET

Al Ain Mall

Al Ain Souk

137TH STREET

120TH STREET

Al Ain Rotana

Al Ain Street

Bus Station

Al Ain Oasis

ZAYED BIN SULTAN STREET

AL SALAM STREET

Jahili Fort

Al Ain National Museum & Sultan bin Zayed Fort

SULTAN BIN ZAYED AL AWWAL STREET

Al Ain Palace Museum

AL AIN STREET

Hilton Al Ain

147TH STREET

KHALID BIN SULTAN STREET

0 metres 500

N

Al Ain Zoo (4km)   Jebel Hafeet (28km)   Camel Souk (6km)

AL AIN SOUK

Immediately in front of the bus station. Most stalls/shops open daily approx 8am–noon/1pm & 4/5–8pm (Fri 4/5–8pm only). MAP P.93

Al Ain Souk is home to the city's main meat, fruit and vegetable market. Housed in a long, functional warehouse-style building, the souk is stocked with the usual picturesque piles of produce, prettiest at the structure's west end, where Indian traders sit enthroned amid huge mounds of fruit and vegetables.

AL AIN PALACE MUSEUM

Al Ain St, on the western side of Al Ain Oasis ☏ 03 751 7755, ⊛ bit.ly/AlAinPalace. Sat, Sun & Tues–Thurs 8.30am–7.30pm, Fri 3–7.30pm, closed Mon. Free. MAP P.93

The **Al Ain Palace Museum** occupies one of the various forts around Al Ain owned by the ruling Nahyan family of Abu Dhabi. The sprawling complex is pleasant enough, with rambling, orangey-pink buildings arranged around a sequence of five courtyards and small gardens, although the palace's thirty-odd rooms, including assorted bedrooms, *majlis* and a small school, aren't particularly interesting.

AL AIN OASIS

JAHILI FORT

120th St, off Sultan bin Zayed al Awwal St. Sat, Sun & Tues–Thurs 8.30am–7.30pm, Fri 3–7.30pm, closed Mon. Free. MAP P.93.

Of Al Ain's various mud-brick forts, **Jahili Fort**, built in 1898, is easily the most impressive, with a fine battlemented main tower and a spacious central courtyard. The much-photographed circular tower on the northern side – with four levels of diminishing size, each topped with a line of triangular battlements – probably pre-dates the rest of the fort. Jahili Fort is also home to the excellent little **Mubarak bin London** exhibition, devoted to the life of legendary explorer **Wilfred Thesiger** (1910–2003). Thesiger – or Mubarak bin London (the "Blessed Son of London") as he was known to his Arab friends – stayed at the fort in the late 1940s at the end of one of the two pioneering journeys across the deserts of the Empty Quarter which later formed the centrepiece of *Arabian Sands*, his classic narrative of Middle Eastern exploration.

HILI GARDENS AND ARCHEOLOGICAL PARK

About 8km north of the city. Daily 9am–10pm. Free.

The **Hili Gardens and Archeological Park** is the site of one of the most important archeological sites in the UAE – many finds from here are displayed in the Al Ain Museum, which also provides a good explanation of their significance. The main surviving structure is the so-called "**Hili Grand Tomb**", a circular mausoleum dating from the third century BC, made from large, finely cut and fitted slabs of stones. A quaint carving of two people framed by a pair of long-horned oryx decorates the rear entrance.

AL AIN ZOO

Off Nahyan al Awwal St, around 7km southwest of the centre ☎ 03 782 8188. ⓦ awpr.ae. Daily 9am–8pm. 15dh; children aged 3–12 5dh; under-3s free.

The excellent **Al Ain Zoo** is a guaranteed crowd-pleaser for both kids and adults. There are over four thousand animals here, humanely housed in large open pens spread around the very spacious grounds. Inmates include plenty of African fauna – big cats, giraffes, zebras and rhinos (including rare South African white lions and Nubian giraffes) – along with numerous Arabian animals and birds.

CAMEL SOUK

Off the Oman road, near the Bawadi mall, about 9km from the city centre.

Al Ain's old-fashioned **Camel Souk** (actually just a series of pens in the open desert) is worth a visit, despite being a bit tricky to find, attracting a lively crowd of local camel-fanciers haggling over dozens of dromedaries lined up for sale. The souk is busiest in the

JAHILI FORT

mornings before around 10am, although low-key trading may continue throughout the day. Be aware that there are some very pushy traders here who may demand massively inflated tips for showing you around or allowing you to take photographs of their animals. Always agree a sum in advance: around 20dh should suffice.

JEBEL HAFEET

30km south of Al Ain on the Omani border. Taxis cost around 100dh.

The soaring 1180m **Jebel Hafeet** (or Hafit), the second-highest mountain in the UAE, is a popular retreat for locals wanting to escape the heat of the desert plains. You can drive to the top in half an hour or less along an excellent road, from where there are peerless views over the surrounding Hajar mountains. The outdoor terrace at the *Mercure Grand*

hotel, perched just below the summit, makes a memorable – if often surprisingly chilly – spot for a drink.

DUBAI DESERT CONSERVATION RESERVE

E66 highway, around 50km from Dubai and 75km from Al Ain ⓦ ddcr.org.

For a taste of real, unadulterated UAE desert, it's well worth a visit to the superb **Dubai Desert Conservation Reserve**. The reserve encloses 250 square kilometres of shifting dunes which serve as a refuge for over thirty local mammal and reptile species, including rare and endangered oryx and Arabian mountain gazelle. Tours can be arranged through Arabian Adventures, Lama, Travco and Alpha (see p.117). Alternatively, you can stay in the reserve at the idyllic but wickedly expensive *Al Maha* resort (see p.111).

Café and restaurant

AL DIWAN

Khalifa bin Zayed St ☎ 03 764 4445. Daily 8am–midnight. MAP P.93

Rustic-looking restaurant with very cheery staff and a menu of mainly Lebanese and Iranian classics – grilled

pigeon, kebabs, assorted mezze and a wide selection of (pricier) seafood. Most mains 35–50dh.

THE HUT

Khalifa bin Zayed St ☎ 03 751 6526. Daily 8am–1pm. MAP P.93

This cosy little café serves up a good selection of teas, coffees, juices, cakes and pastries, plus a short menu of sandwiches from as little as 18dh.

Abu Dhabi

The capital of the UAE, Abu Dhabi is the very model of a modern Gulf petro-city: thoroughly contemporary, shamelessly wealthy and decidedly staid. Abu Dhabi's lightning change from obscure fishing village into modern city-state within the past thirty years is perhaps the most dramatic of the region's stories of oil-driven transformation, although for the casual visitor the city is mainly interesting for how it contrasts with its more famous neighbour – an Arabian Washington to Dubai's Las Vegas. Abu Dhabi's two stand-out attractions are the stunning Sheikh Zayed Mosque, one of the world's largest and most extravagant places of Islamic worship, and the ultra-opulent *Emirates Palace Hotel*. Other draws include the memorable new souk at the World Trade Center, and the contrastingly traditional Heritage Village, offering superb views of Abu Dhabi's long waterfront Corniche.

EMIRATES PALACE HOTEL

Corniche Rd West ☎ 02 690 9000, ⓦ emiratespalace.com. MAP P.97

Standing in solitary splendour at the western end of the city is the vast **Emirates Palace Hotel**. Opened in 2005, it was intended to rival Dubai's Burj al Arab and provide Abu Dhabi with a similarly iconic "seven-star" landmark – although in fact the two buildings could hardly be more different. Driveways climb up through the grounds to the main entrance to the hotel, which sits in an elevated position above the sea and surrounding gardens. It's impressively stage-managed, although the quasi-Arabian design is disappointingly pedestrian and the only really unusual thing about the building is its sheer size: 1km in length, 114 domes, 140 elevators, 2000 staff and so on. The **interior** is a lot more memorable, centred on a dazzling central dome-cum-atrium, with vast quantities of marble and huge chandeliers. Non-guests can visit for a meal at one of the numerous restaurants or drop in to *Le Café* for one of the superb afternoon teas (see p.101) – but dress well to avoid being turned away at the gate.

EMIRATES PALACE HOTEL

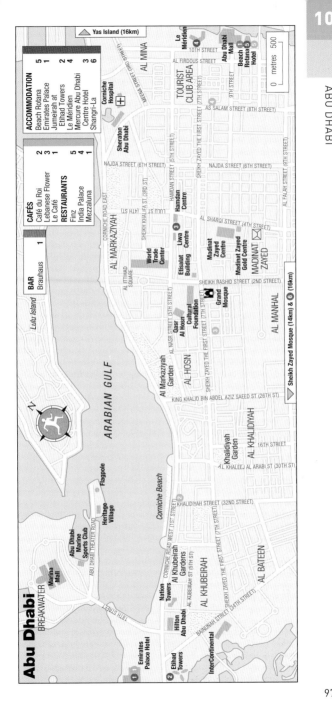

Abu Dhabi

△ Yas Island (16km)

ACCOMMODATION
Beach Rotana 5
Emirates Palace 1
Jumeirah at
Etihad Towers 2
Le Méridien 4
Mercure Abu Dhabi
Centre Hotel 3
Shangri-La 6

CAFÉS
Café du Roi 2
Lebanese Flower 3
Le Café 1
RESTAURANTS
Finz 5
India Palace 4
Mezzaluna 1

BAR
Brauhaus 1

Lulu Island

ARABIAN GULF

BREAKWATER

Marina Mall

Emirates Palace Hotel 1
Etihad Towers 2
InterContinental
Hilton Abu Dhabi
Nation Towers

Abu Dhabi Marine Sports Club
ABU DHABI THEATER ROAD
Heritage Village
Flagpole
Corniche Beach

AL KHUBEIRAH
Al Khubeirah Gardens
AL KUBERAH ST (5TH ST)

CORNICHE ROAD WEST (1ST STREET)

18TH STREET

BAINUNAH STREET (34TH STREET)
SHEIKH ZAYED THE FIRST STREET (7TH STREET)

AL BATEEN

AL KHALIDIYAH STREET (32ND STREET)
Khalidiyah Garden
AL KHALIDIYAH
16TH STREET
AL KHALEEJ AL ARABI ST (30TH ST)

KING KHALID BIN ABDEL AZIZ SAEED ST (26TH ST)

Al Markaziyah Garden

AL HOSN
Qasr Al Hosn
Cultural Foundation

AL NASR STREET (5TH STREET)

Grand Mosque

AL MANHAL

SHEIKH RASHID STREET (2ND STREET)

MADINAT ZAYED
Madinat Zayed Centre
Madinat Zayed Gold Centre

AL MARKAZIYAH
World Trade Center
AL ITTIHAD SQUARE
SHEIKH KHALIFA ST (3RD ST)
LULU ST (4TH ST)

Etisalat Building
Liwa Centre

AL SHARQI STREET (4TH STREET)

Hamdan Centre
HAMDAN STREET (5TH STREET)

NAJDA STREET (6TH STREET)
NAJDA STREET (6TH STREET)

Sheraton Abu Dhabi

MEENA STREET (3RD STREET)

AS SALAM STREET (8TH STREET)

CORNICHE ROAD EAST

Corniche Hospital

AL MINA

AL FIRDOUS STREET

TOURIST CLUB AREA (7TH STREET)

9TH STREET
10TH STREET

Le Méridien
Abu Dhabi Mall
Beach Rotana Hotel

SHEIKH ZAYED THE FIRST STREET (9TH STREET)
AL FALAH STREET (9TH STREET)

▷ Sheikh Zayed Mosque (14km) & 6 (16km)

▷ Sheikh Zayed Mosque (14km) & 6 (16km)

0 metres 500

N

Abu Dhabi transport

Regular express **buses** (5.30am–11.30pm; every 30min; 2hr–2hr 30min; 15dh) run from Al Ghubaiba bus station in Bur Dubai to Abu Dhabi's main bus station, about 3km inland from the city centre. A convenient alternative is to take a **tour** from Dubai. Numerous companies offer Abu Dhabi day-trips (see p.117), generally costing around 220dh. Abu Dhabi's various attractions are very spread out, but there are plenty of metered **taxis** around town (flag fare 3.50dh).

THE CORNICHE

MAP P.97

Driving through Abu Dhabi's suburban sprawl, it's easy not to notice that the city is built on an island – at least until you emerge on the expansive **Corniche**, the sweeping waterfront road that runs for the best part of 5km along Abu Dhabi's western edge. The road is lined by spacious gardens on either side and flanked by a long line of glass-clad high-rises which both encapsulate the city's internationalist credentials and provide Abu Dhabi with its most memorable views.

HERITAGE VILLAGE

Breakwater ☎ 02 681 4455, ⓦ bit.ly /UAE_Heritage_Village. Sat–Thurs 9am–5pm, Fri 3.30–9pm. Free. MAP P.97

Dramatically situated on the Breakwater – a small protuberance of reclaimed land

jutting out from the southern end of the Corniche – the **Heritage Village** offers a slice of traditional Abu Dhabi done up for visiting coach parties. The "village" consists of picturesque *barasti* huts and a small (seldom open) **museum**, and has spectacular views over the water to the Corniche. Opposite the museum is a string of **workshops** where local artisans – carpenters, potters, brass-makers and so on – can sometimes be seen at work. The so-called "traditional market", however, is basically just a few ladies flogging cheap handicrafts out of a line of huts.

MARINA MALL

Marina Village, Breakwater ⓦ marinamall.ae. Sat–Thurs 10am–10pm, Fri 2–10pm. MAP P.97

Dominating the centre of the Breakwater, the large **Marina Mall** is an attractive modern complex built around a series of

THE CORNICHE

tented courtyards and fountains. It's one of the city's two top shopping destinations, along with the glitzy Abu Dhabi Mall on the opposite side of town. Shopping aside, the mall's main attraction is its views of the long string of the high-rises lining the Corniche, best appreciated from the soaring **Burj al Marina** tower at the back of the mall. You can visit for the price of an expensive drink at the 41st-floor *Colombiano* coffee shop.

WORLD TRADE CENTER SOUK

QASR AL HOSN AND AROUND

Al Nasr St (5th St) Ⓦ bit.ly/Qasr-al-Hosn. MAP P.97

More or less at the very centre of Abu Dhabi sits **Qasr Al Hosn** ("The Palace Fort"), the oldest building in Abu Dhabi. The fort started life around 1761 as a single round watchtower built to defend the only freshwater well in Abu Dhabi, and was subsequently expanded, serving as the residence of Abu Dhabi's ruling Al Nahyan family right up until 1966. Under renovation again at the time of writing, it was due to reopen as a major new museum, although no one seems to know when.

WORLD TRADE CENTER AND AROUND

Between Al Ittihad Square and Sheikh Khalifa St (3rd St) Ⓦ wtcad.ae. Souk Sat 10am–11pm, Sun–Thurs 10am–10pm, Fri 3–11pm. MAP P.97

The huge new **World Trade Center**, topped by a pair of shiny cylindrical skyscrapers, is one of the city's most interesting new developments. The Center's main attraction is its marvellous new **souk** (officially known as the "World Trade Center Central Market"), designed by Foster & Partners and offering a memorable

postmodern take on the traditional Arabian bazaar. There are several handicrafts and souvenir shops, and others dedicated to honey and spices.

On the southwestern side of the World Trade Center, **Al Ittihad Square** (also spelt Etihad, meaning "Union") is home to an arresting sequence of oversized sculptures, including a vast cannon, enormous perfume bottle and gargantuan coffeepot – an endearingly quirky contrast to the drab surrounding architecture.

DOWNTOWN ABU DHABI

MAP P.97

The area immediately east of Sheikh Rashid Street (2nd St) is the heart of downtown Abu Dhabi, and where you'll find the city's liveliest street life. The parallel **Hamdan Street** and **Sheikh Zayed the First Street** are the two major thoroughfares, each lined with identikit office blocks stacked tightly together like Lego bricks. Just south of the latter, the **Madinat Zayed Gold Centre** is Abu Dhabi's low-key equivalent to Dubai's Gold Souk, with two floors of jewellery shops selling traditional and modern designs.

SHEIKH ZAYED MOSQUE

SHEIKH ZAYED MOSQUE

15km from central Abu Dhabi, between Al Ain and Al Khaleej al Arabi roads (around 30dh by taxi) ☎ 02 441 6444, ⓦ szgmc.ae/en. Sat–Thurs 9am–10pm, Fri 4.30–10pm (interior closed for about 30min during prayers; check ⓦ szgmc.ae/en/mosque-opening-hours for times). Free guided tours: Sun–Thurs 10am, 11am & 4.30pm, Fri 4.30pm & 8pm, Sat 10am, 11am, 2pm, 4.30pm & 8pm.

The mighty **Sheikh Zayed Mosque** dominates all landward approaches to the city, its snowy-white mass of domes and minarets visible for many kilometres around. Completed in 2007, it's one of the world's biggest – and certainly the most expensive, having taken twelve years to build at a cost of around US$500 million. It's also unusual in being one of only two mosques in the UAE **open to non-Muslims**.

The huge **exterior** is classically plain, framed by four 107m-high minarets and topped with some eighty domes. Entrance to the mosque is through a vast **courtyard** – capable of accommodating some 40,000 worshippers – flanking one side of which is the vast **prayer hall**, a spectacular piece of contemporary Islamic design. The hall is home to the world's largest carpet and biggest chandelier, although it's not the world records which impress so much as the extraordinary muted opulence of the design, with every surface richly carved and decorated.

YAS ISLAND

About 30–35km from central Abu Dhabi; access either from the Dubai highway or along the road via Saadiyat Island.

On the outermost edges of the city, not far from the airport, **Yas Island** is now home to several of the city's key tourist attractions. Fast cars are the principal order of the day here thanks to the presence of the **Yas Marina Circuit** (ⓦyasmarina circuit.com), which hosts the annual Abu Dhabi F1 Grand Prix along with various other races and activities.

If you fancy a bit of Formula 1 action yourself, head to the jaw-droppingly huge **Ferrari World** (ⓦferrariworldabudhabi .com) theme park just down the road, offering a range of rides for hard-core adrenaline junkies and dedicated *tifosi*. Other attractions elsewhere on the island include the Kyle Phillips-designed **Yas Links** golf course (ⓦyaslinks.com) and the **Yas Waterworld** (ⓦyaswater world.com) theme park.

Accommodation in Abu Dhabi is covered on p.111.

Cafés

CAFÉ DU ROI

Al Hana Plaza, Corniche Rd West
☎ 02 681 6151, ⓦ cafeduroi.com.
Daily 6.30am–12.30am. MAP P.97

Popular and long-established French-style café with Filipina waitresses and a largely Emirati clientele. There's a choice of indoor and outdoor seating, a long menu of snacks and light meals (from 30dh) and the best coffee in this part of town.

LEBANESE FLOWER

Off 26th St ☎ 02 665 8700. Daily
7.30am–3am. MAP P.97

This enduringly popular restaurant is the best place in the city to fill up on inexpensive Middle Eastern food, with a well-prepared range of fish and meat grills, kebabs (35–50dh) and mezze.

LE CAFÉ

Emirates Palace Hotel, Corniche Rd West
☎ 02 690 7999, ⓦ emiratespalace.com.
Daily 6.30am–1am. MAP P.97

The *Emirates Palace*'s beautiful foyer café makes a memorable setting for one of the Middle East's most sumptuous afternoon teas; choose either traditional English or Arabian style (served 2–6pm; 275dh).

Restaurants

FINZ

Beach Rotana Hotel, 10th St, Tourist Club Area ☎ 02 697 9350, ⓦ rotana.com /beachrotana. Daily 12.30–3.30pm & 7–11.30pm. MAP P.97

One of the best seafood restaurants in town, occupying an unusual A-frame wooden dining room and terrace overlooking the water. The menu features a wide selection of fish and seafood, ranging from old favourites such as sole meunière to more elaborate creations like red mullet with truffle quinoa. Mains from 140dh.

INDIA PALACE

As Salam St, Tourist Club Area ☎ 02 644 8777, ⓦ indiapalace.ae. Daily noon–midnight. MAP P.97

Long-established and pleasantly old-fashioned Indian restaurant, serving up a big spread of tasty and very reasonably priced North Indian meat, seafood and veg offerings. Veg mains from 25dh, non-veg from 35dh.

MEZZALUNA

Emirates Palace Hotel, Corniche Rd West
☎ 02 690 7999, ⓦ emiratespalace.com. Daily
12.30–3pm & 7–11pm. MAP P.97

One of the more affordable of the *Emirates Palace*'s string of upmarket eating venues, serving traditional Italian and Mediterranean cuisine. Mains 100–225dh.

Bar

BRAUHAUS

Beach Rotana Hotel, 10th St, Tourist Club Area ☎ 02 697 9000, ⓦ rotana.com /beachrotana. Sun–Wed 4pm–1am, Thurs–Sat noon–1am. MAP P.97

This convivial pub-cum-restaurant makes a surprisingly convincing stab at an authentic Bavarian *bierkeller*, with speciality German beers on tap or by the bottle and a good range of food to soak it all up with, served to the accompaniment of Bavarian marching bands and other Teutonic sounds. Very popular, so arrive early if you want to bag a seat.

Accommodation

Dubai has a vast range of accommodation, much of it aimed squarely at big spenders. At the top end of the market, the city has some of the most stunning hotels on the planet, from the futuristic Burj al Arab – the world's first "seven-star" hotel – to traditional Arabian-themed palaces such as *Al Qasr* and the *One&Only Royal Mirage*, and suave modern city hotels like *Raffles* and *Grosvenor House* – as well as the vast *Atlantis* mega-resort. There are plenty of mid-range options scattered across the city, too, although virtually all establishments in this price range tend towards the functional and characterless, providing comfortable lodgings but not much else. There's no real budget accommodation in Dubai, and you won't find a double room anywhere in the city for much less than about 250dh (US$70), or a single for much under 200dh (US$55). The good news is that stringent government regulations and inspections mean standards are reliable even at the cheapest hotels – all are scrupulously clean and fairly well maintained, and come with en-suite bathroom, plenty of hot water, satellite TV and fridge.

Bur Dubai

ARABIAN COURTYARD > Al Fahidi St. Al Fahidi metro ☎ 04 351 9111, Ⓦ arabiancourtyard.com. MAP P.34, POCKET MAP M12. In a brilliantly central location opposite the Dubai Museum, this attractive four-star is a distinct cut above the other mid-range places in Bur Dubai – and usually excellent value too. Decor features a nice mix of modern and Arabian styles, while facilities include a small gym and spa – though the pool is tiny. **650dh**

FOUR POINTS SHERATON > Khalid Bin al Waleed Rd. Al Fahidi metro ☎ 04 397 7444, Ⓦ fourpoints.com/burdubai. MAP P.34, POCKET MAP M13. Understated but very comfortable four-star with nicely furnished rooms in simple international style and good facilities including a gym, (smallish) swimming pool, the excellent

Antique Bazaar restaurant and the cosy *Viceroy Bar* (see p.41). **600dh**

ORIENT GUEST HOUSE > Bastakiya. Al Fahidi metro ☎ 04 353 4448, Ⓦ orientguesthouse.com. MAP P.34, POCKET MAP N12. Cosy heritage hotel (albeit not quite as atmospheric as the nearby *XVA*), occupying an old Bastakiya house. There are eleven rooms attractively decorated with old wooden furniture and four-poster beds. B&B **700dh**

TIME PALACE HOTEL > Just off Al Fahidi St. Al Ghubaiba metro ☎ 04 353 2111, Ⓦ time-palace.com. MAP P.34, POCKET MAP M11. The most consistently reliable budget hotel in Bur Dubai, with spacious and very well-maintained rooms in an unbeatable location just up from the main entrance to the Textile Souk. Tends to get booked up well in advance, so reserve early. **250dh**

Room rates

Hotels in all price ranges chop and change their room rates constantly according to the time of year and demand, so a hotel may be brilliant value one week, and a rip-off the next. The rates given in our reviews are only a very rough guide to average prices; actual costs may sometimes be significantly lower or higher, with price fluctuations of up to 100 percent at the same property quite common. Prices usually (but not always) depend on the **season**. In general, they're highest during the cool winter months from November to February (especially during the Dubai Shopping Festival), and cheapest in high summer (June to August), when rates at some places can tumble by thirty percent or more. **Taxes** (a ten percent service charge and a ten percent municipality tax) are sometimes included in the quoted rate, but not always, so check when booking or you might find yourself suddenly having to cough up an extra twenty percent. All the prices given in the reviews below are for the **cheapest double room in high season** (excluding Christmas and New Year), inclusive of all taxes.

XVA > Bastakiya. Al Fahidi metro ☎ 04 353 5383, Ⓦ xvahotel.com. MAP P.34, POCKET MAP N12. Atmospheric hotel-cum-café (see p.40) with nine rooms tucked away around the back of a fine old Bastakiya house. Rooms are on the small side but brimming with character, featuring Arabian furnishings, slatted windows and four-poster beds, plus captivating views over the surrounding wind towers. B&B **650dh**

Deira

AHMEDIA HERITAGE GUEST HOUSE > Old Baladiya Rd. Al Ras metro ☎ 04 225 0085, Ⓦ ahmediaguesthouse.com. MAP P.43, POCKET MAP N11. Attractive heritage hotel in a very central but peaceful location right next to Al Ahmadiya School, with fifteen rooms attractively done up with traditional wooden furniture and four-poster beds. Free wi-fi. B&B **600dh**

FLORIDA INTERNATIONAL > Opposite Al Sabkha Bus Station, Al Sabkha Rd. Baniyas Square metro ☎ 04 224 7777, Ⓦ florahospitality .com. MAP P.43, POCKET MAP O12. One of Deira's better budget hotels, right in the heart of the downtown action. Rooms (all with wi-fi; 30dh/day) are nicely furnished for the price, and

decent soundproofing means they're reasonably quiet despite the location on a busy main road. **450dh**

HILTON DUBAI CREEK > Baniyas Rd. Al Rigga metro ☎ 04 227 1111, Ⓦ hilton.com/dubai. MAP P.43, POCKET MAP N4. Deira's smartest hotel, with chrome-clad public areas and stylish, well-equipped rooms decorated in minimalist whites and creams; most also have grand Creek views. There's also a health club, a small rooftop pool and the excellent *Table 9* restaurant (see p.49). **1100dh**

LA PAZ > Souk Deira St. Al Ras metro ☎ 04 226 8800, Ⓔ lapazhtl@emirates .net.ae. MAP P.43, POCKET MAP O11. This "family hotel" is perhaps the quietest of the guesthouses clustered around the entrance to the Gold Souk. Rooms are a bit old-fashioned, but perfectly clean and comfortable, and rates are often among the cheapest in the city (including bargain singles at 180dh). **280dh**

LANDMARK GRAND > Al Rigga Rd, opposite Al Ghurair Mall. Union metro ☎ 04 250 1111, Ⓦ landmarkhotels .net. MAP P.43, POCKET MAP O3. Well-run four-star – nothing terribly exciting, but offering comfortable, modern rooms close to the city centre and metro at a reasonable price, plus a health club and rooftop pool. **550dh**

RADISSON BLU DUBAI DEIRA > **CREEK** Baniyas Rd. Union metro ☎ 04 222 7171, Ⓦ radissonblu.com /hotel-dubaidowntown. MAP P.43, POCKET MAP O13. The oldest five-star in the city, this *grande dame* of a hotel still has plenty going for it: an extremely central location, a good spread of restaurants and a scenic position right on the Creek, of which all rooms have a view. Generally excellent value. **850dh**

SHERATON DUBAI CREEK > Baniyas Rd. Union metro ☎ 04 228 1111, Ⓦ sheraton.com/dubai. MAP P.43, POCKET MAP N3. This old-fashioned five-star enjoys a scenic creekside setting and opulent public areas with lots of shiny white marble. Roughly half the rooms have Creek views (the higher the better), though the decor is rather dated and dull, and bathrooms are small. Facilities include a small pool plus good in-house restaurants, including the excellent *Ashiana* (see p.48), while rates are very competitive. **850dh**

The inner suburbs

GRAND HYATT > Sheikh Rashid Rd, Oud Metha. Dubai Healthcare City metro ☎ 04 317 1234, Ⓦ dubai.grand .hyatt.com. MAP P.52, POCKET MAP L7. This colossus of a hotel is grand in every sense – the vast atrium alone could easily swallow two or three smaller establishments, while facilities include four pools, spa, kids' club, gym and fourteen restaurants and bars. The only real drawback is its middle-of-nowhere location, although it is conveniently close to the metro and major roads. **1200dh**

JUMEIRAH CREEKSIDE HOTEL > Sheikh Rashid Rd, Garhoud. GGICO metro ☎ 04 230 8555, Ⓦ jumeirah.com. MAP P.52, POCKET MAP N6. Sleek new five-star – although it's not actually by the side of the Creek. Rooms are nicely done up in funky reds and whites (with fine views from higher floors), and there are a pair of pools and spa. Rates include free access to Wild Wadi water park and the private Madinat Jumeirah beach, with free shuttle bus provided. **1000dh**

PARK HYATT > Dubai Creek Golf and Yacht Club, Garhoud. Deira City Centre metro ☎ 04 602 1234, Ⓦ dubai.park .hyatt.com. MAP P.52, POCKET MAP N6. Alluring five-star set in a beautiful complex of quasi-Moroccan-style buildings surrounded by extensive grounds with plenty of palm trees. Rooms (some with fine Creek views) are unusually large, while facilities include a big pool and the superb Amara spa, plus the *Thai Kitchen* restaurant and attractive *The Terrace* marina-side bar (see p.57). **1700dh**

RAFFLES > Sheikh Rashid Rd, Oud Metha. Dubai Healthcare City metro ☎ 04 324 8888, Ⓦ raffles.com/dubai. MAP P.52, POCKET MAP L6. Vying with the *Park Hyatt* for the title of Dubai's finest city-centre hotel, the spectacular *Raffles* is designed in the form of an enormous postmodern pyramid, with a beautifully executed blend of Egyptian and Asian styling. Rooms feature silky-smooth contemporary decor and fine city views, while facilities include a good selection of eating and drinking establishments, a big pool and extensive grounds. **1700dh**

Sheikh Zayed Road and Downtown Dubai

THE ADDRESS DOWNTOWN DUBAI > Sheikh Mohammed bin Rashid Blvd (Emaar Blvd). Burj Khalifa/Dubai Mall metro ☎ 04 436 8888, Ⓦ theaddress .com. MAP P.60, POCKET MAP E5. OTT five-star occupying a huge high-rise directly opposite the Burj Khalifa. The interior is one of Dubai's most extravagant pieces of interior design, while facilities include a big range of in-house eating and drinking options, including the spectacular *Neos* bar (see p.67) on the 63rd floor. There's also a lavish spa, kids' club and a lovely infinity pool. **1800dh**

ARMANI HOTEL > Floors 5–8 & 38–39, Burj Khalifa. Burj Khalifa/ Dubai Mall metro ☎ 04 888 3888, Ⓦ armanihotels.com. MAP P.60, POCKET MAP E4. Located in the iconic Burj Khalifa, this was the world's first Armani hotel when it opened in 2010. The whole place is kitted out in furnishings from Giorgio's Casa Armani homeware range – all muted whites, greys, browns and blacks. Facilities include a string of fine eating and drinking venues (see p.64), a cool spa and pool. **2650dh**

DUSIT THANI > Sheikh Zayed Rd. Financial Centre metro ☎ 04 343 3333, ⓦ dusit.com. MAP P.60, POCKET MAP F4. Thai-owned and styled five-star combining serene interior design and ultra-attentive service. Rooms are stylishly decorated in soothing creams and browns, while facilities include the excellent *Benjarong* restaurant (see p.64). **1000dh**

FAIRMONT > Sheikh Zayed Rd. World Trade Centre metro ☎ 04 332 5555, ⓦ fairmont.com. MAP P.60, POCKET MAP H3. One of the most stylish hotels hereabouts, huddled around a soaring glass-and-steel atrium illuminated with multicoloured splashes of changing light. Rooms are beautifully furnished with soothing cream decor, while the whole of the ninth floor is given over to leisure facilities, including a sumptuous spa and sunset and sunrise pools on opposite corners of the building. **1500dh**

H HOTEL > Sheikh Zayed Rd ☎ 04 501 8888, ⓦ h-hotel.com. MAP P.60, POCKET MAP J3. Stylish, modern five-star with suave contemporary design spiced up with discreet Arabian styling. Rooms are well equipped, and there are some good places to eat and drink, including the super-cool *Okku*. Competitively priced, and sometimes a real bargain. **1250dh**

IBIS WORLD TRADE CENTRE > Sheikh Zayed Rd. World Trade Centre metro ☎ 04 332 4444, ⓦ ibishotel.com. MAP P.60, POCKET MAP H4. One of the city's best bargains during quiet periods; rates can fall dramatically at weekends. Rooms are small but comfortable (with nice views from higher ones), and guests can use the fitness centre and pools at the adjacent *Novotel* for a small fee. **500dh**

JUMEIRAH EMIRATES TOWERS > Sheikh Zayed Rd. Emirates Towers metro ☎ 04 330 0000, ⓦ jumeirahemiratestowers.com. MAP P.60, POCKET MAP G4. Occupying the smaller of the two iconic Emirates Towers, this exclusive establishment is generally rated the top business hotel in the city, catering mainly to senior execs on expense accounts. Rooms appear designed to calm the nerves of stressed-out CEOs, with muted colours and soothingly understated furnishings, and there's also a dedicated ladies' floor, plus a good-sized pool and health club. **1500dh**

AL MANZIL > Sheikh Mohammed bin Rashid Blvd (Emaar Blvd), Old Town. Burj Khalifa/Dubai Mall metro ☎ 04 428 5888, ⓦ almanzilhotel.ae. MAP P.60, POCKET MAP E5. Stylish little hotel with an engaging mix of traditional Arabian styling and quirky contemporary touches. Rooms are on the small side, although there's a decent spread of amenities including a reasonable-sized pool and the pleasant *Nezesaussi* sports-themed pub-restaurant. The nearby *Qamardeen* hotel (☎ 04 428 6888, ⓦ qamardeenhotel.ae), run by the same company, is very similar. **1250dh**

AL MUROOJ ROTANA > Financial Centre Rd ☎ 04 321 1111, ⓦ rotana.com; Financial Centre metro. MAP P.60, POCKET MAP F4. In a handy location between Sheikh Zayed Rd and the Dubai Mall, this sprawling five-star feels more like a traditional resort than a business hotel. Outside, the extensive, attractively landscaped gardens are dotted with lively restaurants and bars, including the ever-popular *Double Decker* pub (see p.66). Inside there's plenty of contemporary style, with spacious and attractively furnished rooms, some with excellent Burj Khalifa views. **1250dh**

THE PALACE > Sheikh Mohammed bin Rashid Blvd (Emaar Blvd), Old Town. Burj Khalifa/Dubai Mall metro ☎ 04 428 7888, ⓦ theaddress.com/en/hotel /the-palace-downtown-dubai. MAP P.60, POCKET MAP E5. Opulent, Arabian-themed "city-resort" with lavish, quasi-Moroccan styling and a perfect lakeside view of the Dubai Fountain and Burj, best enjoyed from the fine in-house *Thiptara* restaurant (see p.65). Facilities include a superb spa and large lakeside pool. **1750dh**

RITZ-CARLTON > Dubai International Financial Centre. Emirates Towers metro ☎ 04 372 2222, Ⓦ ritzcarlton .com. MAP P.60, POCKET MAP G4. Swanky new five-star aimed at visitors to the adjacent DIFC – good for business, and not bad for pleasure either, if you don't mind the hefty price tag. The whole place is constructed on a palatial scale, with unusually spacious rooms – beautifully kitted out with gorgeous pale yellow furnishings and all mod cons – and extensive facilities including indoor and outdoor pools, spa, gym and a good spread of restaurants. **1800dh**

SHANGRI-LA > Sheikh Zayed Rd. Financial Centre metro ☎ 04 343 8888, Ⓦ shangri-la.com. MAP P.60, POCKET MAP F4. The most stylish hotel on Sheikh Zayed Rd, the *Shangri-La* is pure contemporary class – a beguiling mix of Zen-chic and Scandinavian-cool. Rooms come with smooth pine finishes, beautiful artworks and mirrors everywhere, while leisure facilities include one of the biggest pools in this part of town plus several excellent restaurants. **1500dh**

TOWERS ROTANA > Sheikh Zayed Rd. Financial Centre metro ☎ 04 343 8000, Ⓦ rotana.com. MAP P.60, POCKET MAP G3. This shiny four-star is usually one of the cheaper Shekih Zayed Rd options – a bit run-of-the-mill compared to other nearby places but with comfortable rooms and amenities including a couple of decent in-house restaurants and the ever-popular *Long's Bar* (see p.67). **900dh**

Jumeirah

DUBAI MARINE BEACH RESORT > Jumeirah Rd, near Jumeirah Mosque ☎ 04 346 1111, Ⓦ dxbmarine.com. MAP P.69, POCKET MAP H1. This pocket-sized resort is the only five-star in Dubai where you can be on the beach but also within easy striking distance of the old city. The central location means that facilities don't compare with places further south, although the resort scores highly for its lively collection of bars and restaurants, including *Sho Cho* and *Boudoir* (see p.71). **1300dh**

The Burj al Arab and around

BURJ AL ARAB > ☎ 04 301 7777, Ⓦ burj-al-arab.com. MAP P.73, POCKET MAP K15. A stay in this staggering hotel (see p.72) is the ultimate Dubaian luxury. The "seven-star" facilities include fabulous split-level deluxe suites (the lowest category of accommodation – there are no ordinary rooms here), arrival in a chauffeur-driven Rolls and your own butler, access to the superlative Assawan Spa, a handful of spectacular restaurants and bars (see p.78 & p.79) and a fabulous stretch of beach. **9700dh**

DAR AL MASYAF > Madinat Jumeirah ☎ 04 366 8888, Ⓦ madinatjumeirah .com. MAP P.73, POCKET MAP J16. A more intimate and upmarket alternative to the Madinat Jumeirah's big two hotels, *Dar al Masyaf* consists of a chain of modest, low-rise private villas scattered around the edges of the Madinat complex within extensive, palm-studded gardens. Each villa contains a small number of rooms, sharing an exclusive pool and decorated in the deluxe Arabian manner of *Al Qasr* and *Mina A'Salam*, whose myriad facilities they share. **2800dh**

IBIS > 2A St, near the Mall of the Emirates. Mall of the Emirates metro ☎ 04 382 3000, Ⓦ ibishotel.com. MAP P.73, POCKET MAP J18. This cheery little no-frills hotel is usually the best bargain in southern Dubai, with superb-value rooms and a decent location on the south side of the Mall of the Emirates. There's another Ibis nearby, *Al Barsha* (☎ 04 399 6699), about 1.5km further south next to Sheikh Zayed Rd, which is often even cheaper, though the location is unappealing. **400dh**

JUMEIRAH BEACH HOTEL > Jumeirah Rd ☎ 04 348 0000, Ⓦ jumeirahbeachhotel.com. MAP P.73, POCKET MAP L15. Famous old Dubai landmark (see p.74), and still an excellent place to stay, with a vast range of facilities including over twenty restaurants, seven pools, diving centre – plus jaw-dropping views of the adjacent Burj al Arab. It's particularly good for families, with the Sinbad kids' club, spacious grounds and a fine stretch of beach with plenty of watersports available; guests also get unlimited access to Wild Wadi next door. **2800dh**

MINA A'SALAM > Madinat Jumeirah ☎ 04 366 8888, Ⓦ madinatjumeirah .com. MAP P.73, POCKET MAP K15. Part of the stunning Madinat Jumeirah complex, *Mina A'Salam* ("Harbour of Peace") shares the Madinat's Orientalist styling, with beautifully furnished rooms featuring traditional Arabian wooden furniture and fabrics. Facilities include a nice-looking stretch of private beach, three pools plus the forty-odd restaurants and bars (and myriad shops) of the Madinat complex outside. **3000dh**

AL QASR > Madinat Jumeirah ☎ 04 366 8888, Ⓦ madinatjumeirah .com. MAP P.73, POCKET MAP K16. This extravagant Arabian-themed hotel looks like something out of a film set, from the opulent public areas to the swanky rooms with show-stopping views, sumptuous Oriental decor and pretty much every luxury and mod con you can imagine. There's also a huge pool and all the facilities of the Madinat complex on your doorstep. **3200dh**

The Palm Jumeirah and Dubai Marina

ATLANTIS > Palm Jumeirah ☎ 04 426 0000, Ⓦ atlantisthepalm.com. POCKET MAP E10. This vast mega-resort (see p.81) is the exact opposite of tasteful, but can't be beaten when it comes to in-house attractions, including a water park, dolphinarium, celebrity-chef restaurants, kicking bars and clubs, luxurious spa and vast swathes of sand. There are also excellent kids' facilities, making it a good place for a (pricey) family holiday, with everything you need under one very large roof, while staying here also gets you free or discounted admission to the otherwise expensive on-site activities. It's not the most peaceful place in town, however, more suited to an up-tempo family holiday than a romantic break. **2000dh**

GROSVENOR HOUSE > Al Sufouh Rd. Dubai Marina metro ☎ 04 399 8888, Ⓦ grosvenorhouse-dubai.com. MAP P.82, POCKET MAP C16. One of Dubai's smoothest hotels, set slightly away from the seafront in a pair of elegantly tapering skyscrapers. The entire hotel is a model of contemporary cool, from the suave public areas right through to the elegantly furnished rooms. Facilities include a pool, two excellent spas, and one of the city's best selections of restaurants and bars (see pp.85–87), while guests also have free use of the beach and facilities at the nearby *Le Royal Méridien*. **1440dh**

HILTON DUBAI JUMEIRAH RESORT > The Walk at Jumeirah Beach Residence. Jumeirah Lake Towers metro ☎ 04 399 1111, Ⓦ hilton.com /dubai. MAP P.82, POCKET MAP B15. This glitzy Hilton boasts lots of shiny metal and carries an air of cosmopolitan chic – more of a city-slicker's beach bolt-hole than family seaside resort. Rooms are bright and cheerfully decorated, although facilities are relatively limited compared to nearby places. Outside there's a medium-sized pool and lovely (though rather small) terraced gardens running down to the sea. **1240dh**

JUMEIRAH ZABEEL SARAY > West Crescent, Palm Jumeirah ☎ 04 453 0000, Ⓦ jumeirah.com. MAP P.82, POCKET MAP C13. Easily the most extravagant of the many hotels to have opened in Dubai in recent years: relatively understated from outside, but a riot of quirky opulence within. Public areas and rooms are designed in lavish quasi-Ottoman style, while the hotel's spectacular array of bars and restaurants ranges through a whole encyclopedia of styles – fake Rajasthani palace (see p.85), faux French chateau, burlesque music hall and sci-fi spaceship – all beautifully done, and good fun besides. Facilities include the vast Talisse Ottoman Spa and in-house cinema, while outside there are beautiful grounds, a gorgeous infinity pool and extensive beach (with kids' club). Rates vary wildly, but are often good value, and can sometimes fall to as little as 1200dh – an absolute snip. **2000dh**

LE MÉRIDIEN MINA SEYAHI > Al Sufouh Rd. Nakheel metro ☎ 04 399 3333, ⓦ lemeridien-minaseyahi.com. MAP P.82, POCKET MAP D15. This venerable old five-star has just emerged from lengthy and long-overdue renovations, and is now looking better than it probably ever did, with nicely updated rooms and public areas – although the main draw remains the hotel's superb grounds and big swathe of beach, where you'll also find the kicking *Barasti* beachside bar (see p.87). **1800dh**

LE ROYAL MÉRIDIEN BEACH RESORT AND SPA > The Walk at Jumeirah Beach Residence. Dubai Marina metro ☎ 04 399 5555, ⓦ leroyalmeridien-dubai .com. MAP P.82, POCKET MAP C15. This large and slightly overblown five-star lacks the style of some other places along the beach although it compensates with its extensive grounds and beach, complete with three larger-than-average pools – excellent for families. Facilities include the ostentatious, Roman-themed Caracalla Spa, a smart gym, tennis and squash courts, a kids' club and a good number of restaurants, including the excellent *Rhodes Twenty10* (see p.86). **1800dh**

ONE&ONLY THE PALM > West Crescent, Palm Jumeirah ☎ 04 440 1010, ⓦ thepalm.oneandonlyresorts .com. MAP P.82, POCKET MAP C14. A haven of intimate, understated luxury amid the burgeoning mega-resorts sprouting up around the Palm in an ever-increasing string of bling, *One&Only The Palm* is small, peaceful and very civilized (apart from the fearsome price tag, although special online offers can sometimes cut rates). The style is quasi-Moorish, with hints of the Alhambra in Granada, and neat gardens lining a gorgeous pool, and there's also a fine spa and almost 500m of private beach. A boat shuttle runs guests over to the mainland from the hotel's own marina, where you'll also find the attractive waterside *101* bar-restaurant (see p.86). **4200dh**

ONE&ONLY ROYAL MIRAGE > Al Sufouh Rd. Nakheel metro ☎ 04 399 9999, ⓦ royalmirage.oneandonlyresorts .com. MAP P.82, POCKET MAP E15. The most romantic hotel in town, this dreamy resort is the perfect *One Thousand and One Nights* fantasy made flesh, with a superb sequence of quasi-Moroccan-style buildings scattered amid extensive, palm-filled grounds. The whole complex is actually three hotels in one: *The Palace*, the *Arabian Court* and the *Residence & Spa*, each a little bit more sumptuous (and expensive) than the last. Rooms feature Arabian decor, reproduction antique wooden furniture and colourful rugs, while facilities include a 1km stretch of private beach, four pools, the delectable Oriental hammam-style spa and some of the best restaurants and bars in town (see p.86 & p.87) – all at sometimes surprisingly affordable rates. **2200dh**

RITZ-CARLTON > The Walk at Jumeirah Beach Residence. Dubai Marina metro ☎ 04 399 4000, ⓦ ritzcarlton.com. MAP P.82, POCKET MAP B15. Set in a low-rise, Tuscan-style ochre building, this very stylish establishment is one of the classiest and most eye-wateringly expensive in the city. Rooms are spacious, with slightly chintzy decor, while public areas boast all the charm of a luxurious old country house, especially in the sumptuous lobby lounge. There's also a big and very quiet stretch of private beach and gardens, an attractive spa and good kids' facilities. **3000dh**

SHERATON JUMEIRAH BEACH > The Walk at Jumeirah Beach Residence. Jumeirah Lake Towers metro ☎ 04 399 5533, ⓦ sheraton.com/jumeirahbeach. MAP P.82, POCKET MAP A15. The area's most low-key five-star, particularly good for families, with extensive palm-studded gardens and beach and a watersports centre, while kids get their own pool area, playground and day-care club. Usually a bit cheaper than the nearby competition, but still no bargain. **1440dh**

Out of the city

BAB AL SHAMS DESERT RESORT AND SPA > ☎ 04 381 3231, ⓦ meydanhotels.com/babalshams. INSIDE FRONT COVER FLAP. Hidden out in the desert a 45min drive from the airport, this gorgeous resort occupies a wonderfully atmospheric replica Arabian fort, with desert camel- and horseriding or falconry displays the order of the day, rather than lounging on the beach. Rooms are decorated in traditional Gulf style, with rustic ochre walls and Bedouin-style fabrics, while facilities include a magnificent infinity pool and a good selection of restaurants. **1300dh**

DESERT PALM > ☎ 04 323 8888, Ⓦ desertpalm.peraquum.com. INSIDE FRONT COVER FLAP. On the edge of Dubai, around a 20min drive from the city centre, the *Desert Palm* is a pleasantly laidback suburban bolt-hole, surrounded by polo fields, with distant views of the skyscrapers along Sheikh Zayed Rd. Rooms are beautifully designed and equipped with fancy mod cons while facilities include the superb in-house Lime Spa. **1050dh**

AL MAHA DESERT RESORT AND SPA > Dubai Desert Conservation Reserve, Al Ain Rd ☎ 04 832 9900, Ⓦ al-maha .com. Some 60km from Dubai, this very exclusive, very expensive resort occupies a picture-perfect setting amid the pristine Dubai Desert Conservation Reserve (see p.95) – gazelles and rare Arabian oryx can often been seen wandering through the grounds. The resort is styled like a Bedouin encampment, with accommodation in tented suites featuring handcrafted furnishings and artefacts plus small private pools, and stunning views of the surrounding dunes. Activities include falconry, camel treks, horseriding, archery, 4WD desert drives and guided nature walks; or you can just relax in the resort's serene spa. Full board (including two desert activities per day) around **6500dh**

Abu Dhabi

BEACH ROTANA > 10th St, Tourist Club Area ☎ 02 697 9000, Ⓦ rotana .com/beachrotana. MAP P.97. Smart modern resort-style hotel in the so-called Tourist Club Area, one of Abu Dhabi downtown's liveliest areas. Rooms are spacious and attractively styled, and there's a nice stretch of waterfront beach

and gardens, plus an excellent spread of places to eat and drink. **1000dh**

EMIRATES PALACE > Corniche Rd West ☎ 02 690 9000, Ⓦ emiratespalace.com. MAP P.97. Abu Dhabi's landmark hotel (see p.96) is the favoured residence of visiting heads of state and assorted celebrities, with every luxury you could think of, including lots of swanky restaurants and a vast swathe of beach. Rates aren't always as crushingly expensive as you might expect – check the website for offers. **1500dh**

JUMEIRAH AT ETIHAD TOWERS > Etihad Towers, Corniche Rd West ☎ 02 811 5555, Ⓦ bit.ly/Jumeirah_Etihad. MAP P.97. Swanky new hotel occupying one of the five futuristic skyscrapers of the landmark Etihad Towers development – a cutting-edge alternative to the staid *Emirates Palace* opposite. Rooms are large, luxurious and full of state-of-the-art mod cons, while facilities include three pools, private beach and a serene spa. **1200dh**

LE MÉRIDIEN > 10th St, Tourist Club Area ☎ 02 644 6666, Ⓦ lemeridien .com/abudhabi. MAP P.97. Pleasantly old-fashioned hotel with a vaguely old-world European air and attractive rooms decorated in warm reds and oranges. Plus points include a central location, attractive oceanfront gardens with a smallish bit of beach and a decent collection of restaurants, all at very competitive rates. **550dh**

MERCURE ABU DHABI CENTRE HOTEL > Hamdan St ☎ 02 633 3555, Ⓦ novotel.com. MAP P.97. This no-frills business hotel bang in the city centre is nothing to get excited about, but the rooms are well equipped and comfortable, and rates are often as cheap as anywhere in town. **400dh**

SHANGRI-LA > Qaryat al Beri ☎ 02 509 8888, Ⓦ shangri-la.com /abudhabi. One of the city's most alluring hotels, with gorgeous Arabian Nights decor, huge gardens, four pools, the lovely Chi spa, a gorgeous infinity pool which appears to flow straight into the sea, and wonderful views of the Sheikh Zayed Mosque. **1200dh**

Arrival

Unless you're travelling overland from neighbouring Oman or sailing in on a cruise ship, you'll arrive at Dubai's sparkling modern international **airport** close to the old city centre – at least pending the opening of the new Al Maktoum International Airport (see box below).

The airport (enquiries ☎04 216 6666, ⊛dubaiairport.com) is very centrally located in the district of Garhoud, around 7km from the city centre. There are three passenger terminals: Terminal 1 is where most international flights arrive; Terminal 3 is where all Emirates airlines flights land; and Terminal 2 is used by smaller regional carriers. All three terminals have plenty of ATMs and currency exchange booths, although if you want to rent a car (see p.116), you'll have to head to Terminal 1.

Both Terminal 1 and Terminal 3 have dedicated **metro stations**, offering quick and inexpensive transport into the city (see below). Alternatively, there are plentiful **taxis** (although note that they charge a 20dh flag fare when picking up from the airport, rather than the usual 3dh) and various **buses** (see ⊛dubai-bus.com), although these are only really useful if you're staying in Deira or Bur Dubai and know where you're going; note that (as for the metro) you'll have to buy a Nol card or ticket (see box opposite) before boarding the bus.

Getting around

Dubai is very spread out – it's around 25km from the city centre down to Dubai Marina – but getting around is relatively straightforward and inexpensive, thanks mainly to the excellent metro system. Taxis are also plentiful, while there are also buses and boats, as well as cheap car rental. Full information about the city's public transport is available on the Roads & Transport Authority (RTA) website at ⊛rta.ae. The RTA also provide an excellent **online travel planner** at ⊛wojhati.rta.ae.

By metro

The **Dubai Metro** (⊛rta.ae) offers a cheap, fast and convenient way of getting around, with state-of-the-art driverless trains and eye-catching modern stations. It consists of two lines: the 52km-long **Red Line**, running from Rashidiya, just south of the airport, down Sheikh Zayed

Al Maktoum Airport

D ue to open for passenger flights at the beginning of 2014, the vast new **Al Maktoum International Airport** (AMIA) is located some distance south of the city, around 15km inland from Jebel Ali port, roughly 22km by road from the marina and 50km from the old city centre. It's designed to supplement the existing Dubai International Airport rather than replace it, meaning that services to the older airport should continue more or less as before, although details of how it will all work in practice are, at present, necessarily thin on the ground. From a practical point of view, however, unless you're staying at Dubai Marina, the old Dubai International Airport is likely to prove a far more convenient place to land than its new rival.

Nol cards

Almost all Dubai's public transport services – **metro**, **buses** and **waterbuses** (but not abras) – are covered by the **Nol** system (wnol .ae). To use any of these forms of transport you'll need to buy a pre-paid Nol card or ticket ahead of travel; no tickets are sold on board metro trains, buses or waterbuses. Cards can be **bought** and **topped up** at any metro station; at one of the machines located at 64 bus stops around the city; or at branches of Carrefour, Spinneys and Redha Al-Ansari Exchange.

There are three types of Nol card; all three are valid for five years and can store up to 500dh worth of credit. The **Silver Card** costs 20dh (including 14dh credit). The **Gold Card** (same price) is almost identical, but also allows users to travel on Gold Class compartments on the metro (see below). The **Blue Card**, aimed squarely at residents, costs 70dh (including 20dh credit). An alternative to the three cards is the **Red Ticket** (a paper ticket, rather than a card). This has been specifically designed for tourists, costs just 2dh and is valid for 90 days, although it has to be pre-paid with the correct fare for each journey and can only be recharged up to a maximum of ten times.

Road to Jebel Ali; and the 22km-long **Green Line**, which arcs around the city centre, running from Al Qusais, north of the airport, via Deira and Bur Dubai and then down to Dubai Healthcare City. **Trains** run every 4–8 minutes, with services beginning at around 5.50am daily except on Fridays, when the metro doesn't start running until 1pm. Last trains leave at around 11am (or around midnight on Thursday & Friday).

All trains have a dedicated carriage for **women and children** (look for the signs above the platform barriers) plus a **Gold Class** compartment at the front of/back of the train – these have slightly plusher seating and decor, although the main benefit is that they're usually fairly empty, meaning that you're pretty much guaranteed a seat.

Fares are calculated according to the distance travelled, ranging from 1.80dh up to a maximum of 5.80dh for a single trip (or from 3.60dh to 11.60dh in Gold Class), or 14dh for an entire day's travel (excepting Gold Class). **Children** under 5 or shorter than 0.9m travel free.

By taxi

Away from areas served by the metro, the only way of getting around Dubai quickly is by **taxi**. There are usually plenty of cabs around at all times of day and night (except in Bur Dubai and Deira during the morning and evening rush hours and after dark). **Fares** are pretty good value: there's a minimum charge of 10dh per ride, with a basic flag fare of 3dh (or 3.50dh 10pm–6am), plus 1.71dh per kilometre. The exception is for taxis picked up from the airport, where a 20dh flag fare is imposed; there's also a 20dh surcharge if you take a taxi into Sharjah. You'll also have to pay a 4dh surcharge if your taxi travels through one of Dubai's four tollgates. **Tips** aren't strictly neces-sary, though many taxi drivers will automatically keep the small change from fares unless you specifically ask for it back.

To **book a cab**, call any of the following: Arabia Taxi (☎800 272 242); Cars Taxi (☎800 22 77 89); Dubai Taxi/Ladies Taxis (☎04 208 0808); Metro Taxi (☎600 566 000); or National Taxi (☎600 54 33 22).

By abra

Despite contemporary Dubai's obsession with modern technology, getting from one side of the Creek to the other in the city centre is still a charmingly old-fashioned experience, involving a trip in one of the hundreds of rickety little boats – or abras – which ferry passengers between Deira and Bur Dubai.

There are two main abra **routes**: from Deira Old Souk Abra Station to Bur Dubai Abra Station, and from Al Sabkha Abra Station to Bur Dubai Old Souk Abra Station. The **fare** is just 1dh. Boats leave as soon as full (meaning, in practice, every couple of minutes), and the crossing takes about five minutes. Abras run from 6am to midnight, and 24hr on the route from Bur Dubai Old Souk to Al Sabkha.

By waterbus

A more sedate but much less atmospheric way of getting across the Creek is aboard a **waterbus** – worth considering if you might have problems hopping on and off an abra, although they otherwise don't have much to recommend them. There are four different **routes**, mainly using the same "stations" as the city's abras, but following slightly different routings, with departures every 30 minutes daily from around 7am to 10pm. The **fare** is 2dh per trip, payable by Nol card or ticket (see box, p.115); tickets aren't sold on board.

By bus

Dubai has a well-developed and efficient network of bus services, though it's mainly designed around the needs of low-paid expat workers so is of only limited use for tourists – most routes cover parts of the city that casual visitors are unlikely to want to reach. Most services originate or terminate at either the **Gold Souk Bus Station** in Deira or **Al Ghubaiba Bus Station** in Bur Dubai (many services call at both). Stops elsewhere are clearly signed. Buses are included in the **Nol ticket scheme**, meaning that you'll need to be in possession of a paid-up Nol card or ticket (see box, p.115) before you get on the bus; tickets aren't sold on board.

Buses to **neighbouring emirates** all leave from Al Ghubaiba bus station in Bur Dubai, with regular services to **Sharjah** (every 20–25min; 45min–1hr 15min depending on traffic; services operate 24hr; 7dh), **Abu Dhabi** (every 30min, 5.30am–11.30pm; 2hr–2hr 30min; 15dh) and **Al Ain** (hourly 6.30am–11.30pm; 1hr 30min–2hr; 15dh). These buses aren't covered by the Nol scheme, and you'll need to buy a ticket at the relevant kiosk in the bus station before boarding.

By car

Renting a car is another option, but comes with a couple of caveats. Driving in Dubai isn't for the faint-hearted: the city's roads are permanently busy and standards of driving wayward. **Navigational difficulties** are another big problem, given the city's ever-evolving layout.

For **car rental** contact any of the following: Avis (wavisuae.ae); Budget (wbudget-uae.com); Europcar (weuropcar-middleeast.com); Hertz (whertzuae.com); Sixt (wsixt-uae .com); Thrifty (wthriftyuae.com).

Tours

Dubai has dozens of identikit tour operators who pull in a regular supply of punters in search of the instant "Arabian" experience. The emphasis is firmly on stereotypical **desert safaris** and touristy dhow **dinner cruises**, although a few operators offer more unusual activities ranging from falconry displays to helicopter rides. **Prices** can vary quite considerably from operator to operator, so it's worth shopping around.

City tours

Generic city tours are offered by all our recommended general tour operators (see box below), but for more original insights you might contact the **Sheikh Mohammed Centre for Cultural Understanding** in Bastakiya (☎04 353 6666, ⓦcultures.ae) which runs interesting tours of Jumeirah Mosque and Bastakiya, along with other cultural events (see p.35). **Wonder Bus Tours** in the BurJuman Centre (☎04 359 5656, ⓦwonderbustours.net) also run innovative city tours, aboard the bizarre-looking Wonder Bus – half bus and half boat – starting off by road and then taking to the Creek. Trips last about 1 hour 30 minutes (including 1hr on the Creek) and cost 140dh (95dh for children aged 3–11; family ticket 440dh).

If you've got the cash you might consider an airborne tour of the city, offering peerless views of the Creek and coast. **Seaplane** tours are offered by Seawings (ⓦseawings .ae), while **helicopter** rides around the city can be arranged by several of the operators listed below, including Arabian Adventures. Both start from around 1250dh per person.

Boat cruises

A more leisurely alternative to the standard Creek crossing by abra is to **charter your own boat** (120dh/hr per boat). Starting from the city centre, in an hour you can probably get down to the Dubai Creek Golf Club and back. To find an abra for rent, head to the nearest abra station and ask around.

Alternatively you could go on one of the ever-popular after-dark Creek **dinner cruises**, which can be booked through any tour operator, as well as many of the city's hotels. Most of these use traditional old wooden dhows, offering the chance to wine and dine on the water as your boat sails sedately up and down the Creek. A number of operators now also offer similar dinner cruises sailing between skyscrapers at Dubai Marina. Standard cruises last two hours and cost anything from around 60dh up to 350dh, depending on which operator you go with, inclusive of a buffet dinner and on-board entertainment.

Classy cruises, using a state-of-the-art, modern boat, are run by **Bateaux Dubai** (☎04 814 5553, ⓦbateauxdubai.com; 350dh), while other cheaper but reliable operators include **Al Mansour Dhow** (☎04 205 7033; 185dh), **Rikks Cruises** (☎04 357 2200, ⓦrikks.net; around 150dh) and the bargain-basement **Cruises Dubai** (☎05 871 7200, ⓦcruisesdubai .net; from 55dh).

Tour operators

Alpha Tours ☎04 294 9888, ⓦalphatoursdubai.com
Arabian Adventures ☎04 303 4888, ⓦarabian-adventures.com
Hormuz Tourism ☎04 228 0663, ⓦhormuztourism.com
Knight Tours ☎04 343 7725, ⓦknighttours.co.ae
Lama Tours ☎04 334 4330, ⓦlama.ae
Orient Tours ☎04 282 8238, ⓦorienttours.ae
Sunflower Tours ☎04 334 5554, ⓦsunflowerdubai.com
Travco ☎04 336 6643, ⓦtravcotravel.ae

Desert safaris

One thing that virtually every visitor to Dubai does at some point is go on a **safari** to see some of the desert scenery surrounding Dubai. Although virtually all tours put the emphasis firmly on cheap thrills and touristy gimmicks, most people find the experience enjoyable, in a rather cheesy sort of way.

The vast majority of visitors opt for one of the endlessly popular **half-day safaris** (also known as "sunset safaris"). These are offered by every tour operator, and though the cost ranges from around 150dh up to 350dh – the more expensive tours generally offering superior service, better-quality food and a wider range of entertainment – the basic ingredients remain the same. Tours are in large 4WDs holding around eight passengers. You'll be picked up from your hotel between 3 and 4pm and then driven out into the desert. The usual destination is an area 45 minutes' drive out of town, opposite the massive dune popularly known as Big Red where you'll enjoy a spot of **dune-bashing** – driving at high speed up and down increasingly precipitous dunes amid great sprays of sand. You might also be given the chance to try your hand at a brief bit of **sand-skiing**. As dusk falls, you'll be driven off to one of the dozens of optimistically named desert "Bedouin camps" where attractions will typically include (very short) camel rides, henna painting, dressing up in Gulf national costume, and having your photo taken with an Emirati falcon perched on your arm. A passable international buffet dinner is then served, after which a belly dancer performs for another half hour or so. The whole thing winds up at around 9.30pm, after which you'll be driven back to Dubai.

Directory

Crime and drugs

Dubai is an exceptionally safe city – although a surprising number of tourists and expats manage to get themselves arrested for various breaches of local law. Violent crime is virtually unknown, and even instances of petty theft, pickpocketing and the like are relatively uncommon. The only time you're ever likely to be at risk is while driving. If you need to **call the police** in an emergency, dial ☏999. You can also contact the police's Tourist Security Department toll-free on ☏800 4438 if you have an enquiry or complaint which you think they could help you with.

You should not on any account attempt to enter (or even transit through) Dubai while in possession of any form of **illegal substance**. The death penalty is imposed for drug trafficking, and there's a mandatory four-year sentence for anyone caught in possession of drugs or other proscribed substances. It's vital to note that this doesn't just mean carrying drugs in a conventional sense, but also includes having an illegal substance in your **blood-stream or urine**, or being found in possession of even **microscopic amounts** of a banned substance, even if invisible to the naked eye. Note that poppy seeds (even in bakery products) are also banned. Dubai's hardline anti-drugs regime also extends to certain **prescription drugs**, including codeine and melatonin, which are also treated as illegal substances. If you're on any form of prescription medicine you're supposed to bring a doctor's letter and the original prescription from home, and to bring no more than three months' supply into the UAE.

Culture and etiquette

Despite its glossy Western veneer and apparently liberal ways, it's important to remember that Dubai is an Islamic state, and that visitors are expected to comply with local cultural norms or risk the consequences.

There are a few simple rules to remember if you want to stay out of trouble. During **Ramadan** remember that between dawn and dusk eating, drinking, smoking or chewing gum in public are a definite no-no, as are singing, dancing and swearing in public (you are, however, free to eat and drink in any of the carefully screened-off dining areas set up in hotels throughout the city, while alcohol is also served discreetly after dark in some places). At any time, public displays of **drunkenness** contravene local law, and could get you locked up. Driving while under any sort of influence is even more of a no-no. Inappropriate public behaviour with members of the opposite sex can result in, at best, embarrassment, or, at worst, a spell in prison. Holding hands or a peck on the cheek is probably just about OK, but any more passionate **displays of affection** are severely frowned upon. **Offensive gestures** are another source of possible danger. Giving someone the finger or even just sticking out your tongue might be considered rude at home but can get you jailed in Dubai.

In terms of general etiquette, except around the hotel pool, **modest dress** is expected of all visitors. Dressing "indecently" is potentially punishable under law (even if actual arrests are extremely rare), although exactly what constitutes indecent attire isn't clearly defined. If you're fortunate enough to spend any time with Emiratis, remember that only the right hand should be used for eating and drinking (this rule also applies in Indian establishments), and don't offer to shake the hand of an Emirati woman unless she extends hers toward you.

Electricity

UK-style **sockets** with three square pins are the norm (although you might occasionally encounter Indian-style round-pin sockets in budget hotels in Bur Dubai and Deira). The city's **current** runs at 220–240 volts AC, meaning that UK appliances will work directly off the mains supply, although US appliances will probably require a transformer.

Embassies and consulates

Foreign embassies are mainly located in the UAE's capital, Abu Dhabi, although many countries also maintain consulates in Dubai.

Australia Consulate-General, Level 25, BurJuman Business Tower, Khalifa bin Zayed Rd, Bur Dubai ☎04 5087 100, ⓦuae.embassy.gov.au.

Canada Consulate-General, 19th Floor, Emirates Towers, Sheikh Zayed Rd ☎04 404 8444, ⓦwww.canada international.gc.ca/uae-eau.

Ireland Embassy, 4th floor, Monarch Hotel Office Tower, 1 Sheikh Zayed Rd (opposite the World Trade Centre) ☎04 329 8382, ⓦembassyofireland.ae.

New Zealand Consulate-General, Suite 1502, 15th Floor, API Tower, Sheikh Zayed Rd ☎04 331 7500, ⓦimmigration.govt.nz/branch/Dubai BranchHome.

South Africa Consulate-General, 3rd Floor, New Sharaf Building, Khaleed bin al Waleed St, Bur Dubai ☎04 397 5222, ⓦsouthafricadubai.com.

UK Embassy, Al Seef Rd, Bur Dubai ☎04 309 4444, ⓦukinuae.fco.gov .uk/en.

US Consulate-General, Corner of Al Seef and Sheikh Khalifa bin Zayed roads, Bur Dubai ☎04 309 4000, ⓦdubai.usconsulate.gov.

Gay and lesbian travellers

Dubai is one of the world's less-friendly gay and lesbian destinations. Homosexuality is illegal under UAE law, with punishments of up to ten years in prison – a useful summary of the present legal situation and recent prosecutions can be found at ⓦen.wikipedia.org/wiki/LGBT_rights_in_the_United_Arab_Emirates. Despite this, the city boasts a very clandestine gay scene, attracting both foreigners and Arabs from even less-permissive cities around the Gulf, although you'll need to hunt hard to find it without local contacts. Relevant websites are routinely censored within the UAE, so you'll probably have to do your online research before you arrive. Useful resources include ⓦgaymiddleeast.com, ⓦfacebook.com/LGBTRights UAE and ⓦgaysdubai.com.

Health

There are virtually no serious **health risks** in Dubai (unless you include the traffic). The city is well equipped with modern hospitals, while all four- and five-star hotels have English-speaking **doctors** on call 24hr. **Tap water** is safe to drink, while even the city's cheapest curry houses and shwarma cafés maintain good standards of **food hygiene**. The only genuine health concern is the **heat**. Summer temperatures regularly climb into the mid-forties, making sunburn, heatstroke and acute dehydration a real possibility, especially if combined with excessive alcohol consumption. Stay in the shade, and drink lots of water.

Emergency numbers

Ambulance ⓣ999
Fire ⓣ997
Police ⓣ999

Pharmacies can be found all over the city, including a number run by the BinSina chain which are open 24hr. There are three main **government hospitals** with emergency departments (more details at ⓦdha.gov.ae): Dubai Hospital, between the Corniche and Baraha Street, Deira (ⓣ04 219 5000); Latifa Hospital (formerly Al Wasl Hospital), Oud Metha Road (just west of Wafi), Oud Metha (ⓣ04 219 3000); and Rashid Hospital, off Oud Metha Road, near Maktoum Bridge, Oud Metha (ⓣ04 219 2000). You'll need to pay for treatment, though cost should be recoverable through your travel insurance. **Private hospitals** with emergency departments include the American Hospital, off Oud Metha Road (opposite the *Mövenpick* hotel), Oud Metha (ⓣ04 336 7777, ⓦahdubai.com), and Emirates Hospital, opposite Jumeirah Beach Park, Jumeirah Beach Road, Jumeirah (ⓣ04 349 6666, ⓦemirateshospital.ae).

Internet

All the better **hotels** provide internet access, either via computers in their business centres or via wi-fi or in-room cable connections. This is sometimes provided free, although is usually chargeable, often at extortionate rates (30dh/hr is common in more upmarket hotels). The city has frustratingly few **internet cafés**. The best area to look is Bur Dubai, which boasts a scattering of small places – try Aimei internet café (daily 8am–midnight; 3dh/hr) on 13c Sikka, behind the *Time Palace* hotel, or Futurespeed (daily 8am–11pm; 10dh/hr) in the BurJuman centre (by the Dôme café). There are also various free wi-fi hotspots around the city operated by the city's two telecom companies, Etisalat (ⓦetisalat.ae) and Du (ⓦdu.ae).

Internet access in Dubai is subject to a certain modest amount of **censorship** including a blanket ban on anything remotely pornographic, plus gambling and dating sites, and pages which are considered religiously or culturally offensive.

Lost property
For major items of lost property, try asking at the nearest local police station. If you accidentally leave something in a taxi, call the RTA Contact Centre on ☎800 9090.

Money
The UAE's currency is the **dirham** (abbreviated "dh" or "AED"), subdivided into 100 fils. The dirham is pegged against the US dollar at the rate of US$1=3.6725dh; other **exchange rates** at the time of writing were £1=5.93dh, €1=4.85dh. **Notes** come in 5dh, 10dh, 20dh, 50dh, 100dh, 200dh, 500dh and 1000dh denominations; there are also 2dh, 1dh, 50 fils and 25 fils coins.

There are plenty of **ATMs** all over the city which accept foreign Visa and MasterCards. All the big shopping malls have at least a few ATMs, as do some large hotels and almost all banks. All will also change **travellers' cheques** and **foreign cash**, and there are also plenty of **moneychangers**, including the reputable Al Ansari Exchange, which has branches all over the city (see ⌨alansariexchange.com/en/branches).

Opening hours
Dubai runs on an Islamic rather than a Western schedule, meaning that the city operates according to a basic **five-day working week** running Sunday to Thursday, with Friday as the Islamic holy day. When people talk about the **weekend** in Dubai they mean Friday and Saturday.

The most important fact to note is that many tourist sites and the Dubai Metro are **closed on Friday morning**, while **banks** usually open Saturday to Wednesday 8am–1pm and Thursday 8am–noon (some also reopen in the afternoon from 4.30–6.30pm). **Shops** in **malls** generally open daily from 10am to 10pm, and until midnight on Friday and Saturday (and sometimes Thursday as well); shops in **souks** follow a similar pattern, though many places close for a siesta between around 1pm and 4pm depending on the whim of the owner. Most **restaurants** open daily for lunch and dinner (although some more upmarket hotel restaurants open for dinner only). **Pubs** tend to open daily from around noon until 2am; **bars** from around 6pm until 2/3am.

Phones
The **country code** for the UAE is ☎971. The **city code** for Dubai is ☎04; Abu Dhabi is ☎02; Sharjah is ☎06; Al Ain is ☎03. To **call abroad from the UAE**, dial ☎00, followed by your country code and the number itself (minus its initial zero). To call Dubai from abroad, dial your international access code, then ☎9714, followed by the local subscriber number (minus the ☎04 city code). For **directory enquiries** call ☎181 (Etisalat) or ☎199 (Du).

Post
The two most convenient **post offices** for visitors are the Al Musalla Post Office (Sat–Thurs 7.30am–3pm) at Al Fahidi Roundabout, opposite the *Arabian Tea House Café* in Bur Dubai; and the Deira Post Office on Al Sabkha Road (Sat–Thurs 7.30am–9pm), near the intersection with Baniyas Road. Airmail letters to Europe, the US and Australia cost 5dh (postcards 3.50dh).

Smoking

Smoking is banned in Dubai in the vast majority of indoor public places, including offices, malls, cafés and restaurants (although it's permitted at most – but not all – outdoor venues, and in bars and pubs. Many **hotels** now provide non-smoking rooms or non-smoking floors – and a few places have banned smoking completely. During Ramadan, never smoke in public places in daylight hours.

Time

Dubai (and the rest of the UAE) runs on **Gulf Standard Time**. This is 4hr ahead of GMT, 3hr ahead of BST, 9hr ahead of North American Eastern Standard Time, 12hr ahead of North American Western Standard Time, 6hr behind Australian Eastern Standard Time, and 8hr behind New Zealand Standard Time. There is no daylight saving time in Dubai.

Tipping and taxes

Room rates at most of the city's more expensive hotels are subject to a ten percent **service charge** and an additional ten percent **government tax**; these taxes are sometimes included in quoted prices, and sometimes not. Check beforehand, or you may find your bill has suddenly inflated by twenty percent. The prices in most restaurants automatically include all relevant taxes and a ten percent service charge (though this isn't necessarily passed on to the waiters themselves); whether you wish to leave an additional **tip** is entirely your decision.

Tourist information

There's a frustrating lack of on-the-ground visitor information in Dubai – and not a single proper tourist office anywhere in the city. You could try ringing the head office of the **Department of Tourism and Commerce Marketing (DTCM**; ☎04 223 0000 or ☎04 282 1111, complaints toll-free on ☎800 7090) or visiting one of their erratically manned information desks at Terminal 1 and Terminal 3 in the airport (both 24hr), and at Deira City Centre, BurJuman, Wafi and Ibn Battuta malls (all daily 10am–10pm), although none is especially useful. Online, the DTCM has two lacklustre official websites (ⓦdubaitourism.ae and ⓦdefinitelydubai.com), although the best resource is the lively *Time Out Dubai*, whether in magazine form – it's published weekly and available at bookshops all over the city – or online (ⓦtimeoutdubai.com). It carries comprehensive listings about pretty much everything going on in Dubai, and is particularly good for information about the constantly changing nightlife scene, including club, restaurant and bar promotions and new openings.

Travellers with disabilities

Dubai is probably the Middle East's most accessible destination. Most of the city's modern **hotels** now make at least some provision for guests with impaired mobility, and many of the city's four- and five-stars now have specially adapted rooms. Quite a few of the city's **malls** also have special

DTCM tourist offices overseas

Australia ☎02 9956 6620, ✉dtcm_aus@dubaitourism.ae.
South Africa ☎011 702 9600, ✉dtcm_sa@dubaitourism.ae.
UK ☎020 7321 6110, ✉dtcm_uk@dubaitourism.ae.
USA ☎212 725 0707, ✉dtcm_usa@dubaitourism.ae.

facilities, including disabled parking spaces and specially equipped toilets. Inevitably, most of the city's older heritage buildings are not accessible (although the Dubai Museum is).

Transportation is fairly well set up. The Dubai Metro incorporates facilities to assist visually and mobility-impaired visitors, including tactile guide paths, lifts and ramps, as well as wheelchair spaces in all compartments, while **Dubai Taxi** (☎04 208 0808) has specially designed vehicles equipped with ramps and lifts. The city's **waterbuses** can also be used by mobility impaired visitors, and staff will assist you in boarding and disembarking. There are also dedicated facilities at the **airport**.

Travelling with children

Dubai has a vast array of attractions for children, although many come with hefty price tags attached. Most of the city's beach hotels have their own in-house **kids' clubs**, providing free childcare (usually catering for ages 4–12), while most larger shopping malls have dedicated kids' play areas. Most hotels can arrange **babysitting** services for a fee. Attractions designed especially for kids include:

Children's City Creek Park, Oud Metha (☎04 334 0808, ⓦchildrencity.ae; Dubai Healthcare City metro). Occupying an eye-catching series of brightly coloured red and blue buildings in Creek Park, Children's City is aimed at kids aged 2–15, with a subtle educational slant and various galleries with fun interactive exhibits and lots of touchscreens covering subjects including physical science, nature, international culture and space exploration. 15dh, children 3–15 years 10dh; under 2s free; family ticket for 2 adults and 2 children 40dh; 5dh park entry fee. Sat–Thurs 9am–8pm, Fri 3–9pm.

Dubai Dolphinarium Creek Park (just inside the park near Gate #1), Oud Metha (☎04 336 9773, ⓦdubaidolphinarium.ae; Dubai Healthcare City metro). Twice-daily shows (Mon–Sat at 11am & 6pm; also Fri & Sat at 3pm; adults 100dh, children 50dh) starring the dolphinarium's three resident bottlenose dolphins and four seals. Alternatively, you can go swimming with the dolphins (2100dh for up to 3 people, 550dh each additional person).

Ferrari World Yas Island, Abu Dhabi (☎02 496 8001, ⓦferrariworld abudhabi.com). The blockbuster attraction at Abu Dhabi's Yas Island (see p.100), the "world's biggest indoor theme park" offers a wide range of Ferrari-themed rides and displays which will appeal both to kids and grown-ups. Adults and children over 1.3m 225dh; under 1.3m 185dh; under-3s free. Daily except Mon 11am–10pm.

KidZania Second floor, Dubai Mall (ⓦkidzania.ae; Burj Khalifa/Dubai Mall metro). Innovative edutainment attraction based on an imaginary city where the kids are in charge. Children get the chance to dress up and roleplay from 75 different grown-up professions and even earn their own money en route. Ages 17+ 95dh; ages 4–16 140dh; ages 2–3 95dh; under 2s free. Daily 10am–9pm.

Sega Republic Second floor, Dubai Mall (ⓦsegarepublic.com; Burj Khalifa/Dubai Mall metro). Huge indoor theme park featuring a range of adrenaline-pumping rides and other amusements for kids of all ages. 160dh for one-day pass (including 10 video games); 220dh for one-day pass (including 200dh credit for games); general admission ticket 10dh, with pay as you go from 15–30dh for individual rides. Daily 10am–11pm (Thurs–Sat until 1am).

Festivals and events

Dubai hosts a number of world-class annual festivals showcasing film, music and the visual arts, while neighbouring Abu Dhabi also stages a number of leading cultural and sporting events. For a complete listing of events in the city, see ⓦdubaicalendar.ae.

DUBAI MARATHON

Mid-Jan ⓦdubaimarathon.org.
Top distance runners battle it out.

DUBAI SHOPPING FESTIVAL

One month in Jan/Feb ⓦdubaievents .ae/en.
Shops citywide offer all sorts of sales bargains, with discounts of up to 75 percent, while the big malls lay on entertainment and children's events.

DUBAI INTERNATIONAL JAZZ FESTIVAL

One week in Feb ⓦdubaijazzfest.com.
Top local and international jazz and pop acts perform at Festival City.

DUBAI DESERT CLASSIC

Four days in Feb ⓦdubaidesertclassic.com.
Major event on the PGA European Tour held at the Emirates Golf Club and attracting leading stars.

DUBAI TENNIS CHAMPIONSHIPS

Two weeks in late Feb/early March
ⓦdubaitennischampionships.com.
Established fixture on the international tennis calendar at the Dubai Tennis Stadium in Garhoud, pulling in top male and female players.

ART DUBAI

Four days in mid-March ⓦartdubai.ae.
Some 75 galleries from around the world exhibit at Madinat Jumeirah.

BASTAKIYA ART FAIR

One week in mid-March ⓦbastakiyaartfair .com.
Held at the same time as Art Dubai, with shows of work in the Bastakiya quarter by up-and-coming artists.

DUBAI WORLD CUP

March ⓦdubaiworldcup.com.
The world's richest horse race, with a massive US$10 million in prize money, held at Meydan Racecourse.

TASTE OF DUBAI

Three days in mid-March ⓦtasteofdubai festival.com.
Live cookery exhibitions at Dubai Media City by local and visiting international celebrity chefs.

ABU DHABI DESERT CHALLENGE

Five days in March/April
ⓦabudhabidesertchallenge.com.
Rally drivers, bikers and quad-bikers race each other across the desert.

TRADITIONAL DHOW RACING

April/May ⓦdimc.ae.
Traditional wooden dhows under sail at the Dubai International Marine Club in Dubai Marina.

DUBAI SUMMER SURPRISES

Mid-June to mid-July ⓦdubaievents.ae /en/dss.
Mainly mall-based event with shopping bargains on offer and lots of live children's entertainment.

RAMADAN

Estimated dates: June 28 to July 27, 2014; June 18 to July 16, 2015; June 6 to July 4, 2016; May 27 to June 24, 2017.
The Islamic holy month of Ramadan is observed with great care in Dubai.

Muslims are required to fast from dawn to dusk, and as a tourist you are expected publicly to observe these strictures (see p.119). Fasting ends at dusk, at which point the city springs to life in a celebratory round of eating, drinking and socializing known as Iftar ("The Breaking of the Fast"). The atmosphere is particularly exuberant during Eid ul Fitr, the day marking the end of Ramadan, which erupts in an explosion of festivity. Precise dates for Ramadan vary according to local astronomical sightings of the moon.

EID AL ADHA

Estimated dates: Oct 4, 2014; Sept 23, 2015; Sept 11, 2016; Sept 1, 2017
Falling approximately 70 days after the end of Ramadan, the "Festival of the Sacrifice" celebrates the willingness of Ibrahim to sacrifice his son Ismail at the command of God.

ABU DHABI F1 GRAND PRIX

Three days in Nov ⓦyasmarinacircuit.com.
The Gulf's premier sporting event, held annually at the spectacular Yas Marina Circuit.

DUBAI WORLD CHAMPIONSHIP

Four days in Nov ⓦdubaiworldchampionship .com.
Held at the Earth course, Jumeirah Golf Estates, this is the showpiece finale of the European Tour's season-long "Race to Dubai".

DUBAI RUGBY SEVENS

Three days in late Nov/early Dec
ⓦdubairugby7s.com.
Annual IRB Sevens World Series tournament at Dubai's Sevens stadium, accompanied by some of the city's most raucous partying.

DUBAI INTERNATIONAL FILM FESTIVAL

One week in mid-Dec ⓦdubaifilmfest.com.
International art-house films, with a particular focus on home-grown work and usually a few well-known celebs in attendance.

NATIONAL DAY

Dec 2
The UAE's independence day is celebrated with a raft of citywide events.

Public holidays

There are seven public holidays in Dubai: two have fixed dates, while the other five shift annually according to the Islamic calendar (falling around 11 days earlier from year to year).

New Year's Day Jan 1.

Milad un Nabi (Birth of the Prophet Mohammed) Estimated dates: Jan 3, 2015; Dec 24, 2015; Dec 12, 2016.

Leilat al Meiraj (Ascent of the Prophet) Estimated dates: May 25, 2014; May 15, 2015; May 4, 2016; April 23, 2017.

Eid ul Fitr (the end of Ramadan; see above) Estimated dates: July 28, 2014; July 17, 2015; July 5, 2016; June 25, 2017.

Eid al Adha (the Festival of the Sacrifice; see above) Estimated dates: Oct 4, 2014; Sept 23, 2015; Sept 11, 2016; Sept 1, 2017.

Al Hijra (Islamic New Year) Estimated dates: Oct 25, 2014; Oct 14, 2015; Oct 2, 2016; Sept 21, 2017.

National Day (see above) Dec 2.

Chronology

c.5000 BC > Earliest human settlement in the southern Gulf.

500–600 AD > The UAE region becomes part of an extensive trade network dominated by the Sassanian (Iranian) empire; settlement of Jumeirah area.

c.630 > Arrival of Islam.

751 and onwards > The southern Gulf experiences a major boom in maritime trade following the shifting of the Islamic caliphate from Damascus to Baghdad.

1580 > First European reference to Dubai, by the Venetian pearl merchant Gaspero Balbi.

1820 > Britain signs series of treaties (or "truces") with various Gulf rulers, whose territories are henceforth known as the Trucial States.

1833 > Around a thousand Bani Yas tribesmen from Abu Dhabi take control of Dubai under the leadership of Maktoum bin Buti.

1835 > Britain formally recognizes Dubai and enters into treaty with it.

1841 > Settlement of Deira begins. Over the next decade the town grows rapidly, attracting a cosmopolitan population of Arabs, Iranians, Indians and Pakistanis.

1894 > Dubai declared a free port by Sheikh Maktoum bin Hasher. Iranian merchants begin arriving in the city.

1929 onwards > Gradual collapse of the pearl trade following the Great Depression and Japanese discovery of artificial pearl culturing.

1958 > Death of Sheikh Saeed, succeeded by his son Sheikh Rashid.

1960 > Dubai International Airport is opened.

1960–61 > The Creek is dredged, establishing Dubai as the southern Gulf's major port.

1963 > The first bridge across the Creek – Maktoum Bridge – is opened.

1966 > Oil is discovered in the offshore Fateh field.

1971 > The British withdraw from the Trucial States, which are re-formed as the United Arab Emirates. Opening of Port Rashid.

1970s and 1980s > Oil revenues are used to diversify Dubai's industrial base and create massive new infrastructure projects, such as Jebel Ali Port and Free Zone (1983), and the World Trade Centre (1979).

1990 > Death of Sheikh Rashid; Sheikh Maktoum becomes ruler of Dubai, though Crown Prince Sheikh Mohammed also exerts increasing influence over the city's development.

1996 > Dubai Shopping Festival held for the first time.

1998 > Opening of the Burj al Arab.

2006 > Death of Sheikh Maktoum; Sheikh Mohammed becomes ruler.

2008 > Credit crunch hits Dubai; emirate teeters on edge of bankruptcy; many major projects cancelled or mothballed.

2010 > Opening of Burj Khalifa, the world's tallest building.

2012 > Plans for ambitious new Mohammed bin Rashid City announced.

Language

Language in Dubai is as complicated as the ethnic patchwork of people who inhabit the city. The city's official language is **Arabic**, spoken by nearly a third of the population, including local Emiratis, other Gulf Arabs and various Arabic-speaking expats from countries like Lebanon, Syria, Jordan and further afield. **Hindi** and **Urdu** are the mother tongues of many of the city's enormous number of Indian and Pakistani expats, although other Indian languages, most notably Malayalam, the native tongue of Kerala, as well as Tamil and Sinhalese (the majority language of Sri Lanka), are also spoken. Other Asian languages are also common, most notably **Tagalog**, the first language of the city's large Filipino community.

In practice, the city's most widely understood language is actually **English** (even if most speak it only as a second or third language), which serves as a link between all the city's various ethnic groups, as well as the principal language of the European expat community and the business and tourism sectors. Pretty much everyone in Dubai speaks at least a little English (ironically, even local Emiratis are now forced to revert to this foreign language in many of their everyday dealings in their own city).

Knowing the ethnic origin of the person you're speaking to is obviously the most important thing if you do attempt to strike out into a foreign tongue – speaking Arabic to an Indian taxi driver or a Filipina waitress is obviously a complete waste of time. The bottom line is that few of the people you come into contact with in Dubai will be Arabic-speakers, except in the city's Middle Eastern restaurants. And unless you're pretty fluent, trying to speak Arabic (or indeed any other language) in Dubai is mainly an exercise in diplomacy rather than a meaningful attempt to communicate, since the person you're addressing will almost certainly speak much better English than you do Arabic (or Hindi, or whatever). Having said that, there's no harm in giving it a go, and the person you're speaking to may be pleasantly entertained by your attempts to address him or her in their own language.

Useful Arabic words and phrases

Hello (formal)	a'salaam alaykum (response: wa alaykum a'salaam)
Hello (informal)	marhaba/ahlan wasahlan
Good morning	sabah al kheer
Good evening	masaa al kheer
Good night (to a man/ woman)	tisbah al kher/ tisbahi al kher
Goodbye	ma'assalama
Yes	na'am/aiwa
No	la
Please (to a man/ woman)	minfadlack/ minfadlick
Excuse me	afwan
Thank you	shukran
You're welcome	afwan
Sorry	afwan
OK	n'zayn
How much?	bikaim?
Do you speak English?	teh ki ingelezi?
I don't speak Arabic	ma ah'ki arabi
I understand	ana fahim (fem: ana fahma)
I don't understand	ana ma fahim (fem: ana ma fahma)
My name is ...	Ismi ...
What is your name?	Sho ismak?
God willing!	Inshallah
I'm British	ana Britani
Irish	Irlandee
American	Amerikanee
Canadian	Canadee
Australian	Ostralee
from New Zealand	Noozeelandee

Where are you from?	min wayn inta?
Where is?	wayn?
in	fi
near/far	gareeb/ba'eed
here/there	hina/hunak
open/closed	maftooh/mseeker
big/small	kabeer/saghir
old/new	kadeem/jadeed
day/night	yoom/layl
today/tomorrow	al yoom/bokra
perhaps	mumkin
No problem	ma fi mushkila
Not possible	mish mumkin
I don't speak Arabic	ma'atkallam arabi (or just la arabiya)
Leave me alone!	Imshi!

NUMBERS

1	wahid
2	ithnayn
3	theletha
4	arba'a
5	khamsa
6	sitta
7	saba'a
8	themanya
9	tissa
10	ashra
20	aishreen
30	thelatheen
40	arba'aeen
50	khamseen
100	maya
1000	elf

Food glossary

The traditional Middle Eastern meal consists of a wide selection of small dishes known as **mezze** (or *meze*) shared between a number of diners. Most or all of the following dishes, dips and other ingredients are found in the city's better Middle Eastern (or "Lebanese", as they are usually described) restaurants and cafés, although note that vagaries in the transliteration from Arabic script to English can result in considerable variations in spelling.

arayes slices of pitta bread stuffed with spiced meat and baked

baba ghanouj all-purpose dip made from grilled aubergine (eggplant) mixed with ingredients like tomato, onion, lemon juice and garlic

burghul cracked wheat, often used as an ingredient in Middle Eastern dishes such as tabbouleh

falafel deep-fried balls of crushed chickpeas mixed with spices; usually served with bread and salad

fatayer miniature triangular pastries, usually filled with either cheese or spinach

fatteh dishes containing pieces of fried or roasted bread

fattoush salad made of tomatoes, cucumber, lettuce and mint mixed up with crispy little squares of deep-fried flatbread

foul madamas smooth dip made from fava beans (*foul*) blended with lemon juice, chillis and olive oil

halloumi grilled cheese

hammour common Gulf fish which often crops up on local menus; a bit like cod

humous crushed chickpeas blended with tahini, garlic and lemon; served as a basic side dish and eaten with virtually everything, from bread and vegetables through to meat dishes

jebne white cheese

kibbeh small ovals of deep-fried minced lamb mixed with cracked wheat and spices

kushari classic Egyptian dish featuring a mix of rice, lentils, noodles, macaroni and fried onion, topped with tomato sauce

labneh thick, creamy Arabian yoghurt, often flavoured with garlic or mint

loubia salad of green beans with tomatoes and onion

moutabal a slightly creamier version of *baba ghanouj*, thickened using yoghurt or tahini

mulukhiyah soup-cum-stew with a characteristically slimy texture, made from boiled *mulukhiyah* leaves

saj Lebanese style of thin, round flatbread

saj manakish (or *mana'eesh*) pieces of *saj* sprinkled with herbs and oil – a kind of Middle Eastern mini-pizza

sambousek miniature pastries, filled with meat or cheese and then fried

sharkaseya chicken served in a creamy walnut sauce

shisha waterpipe (also known as hubbly-bubbly). Tobacco is filtered through the glass water-container at the base of the pipe, and so is much milder (and less harmful) than normal cigarettes. Tobacco is usually available either plain or in various flavoured varieties; the best shisha cafés may have as many as twenty varieties

shish taouk basic chicken kebab, with small pieces of meat grilled on a skewer and often served with garlic sauce

shwarma chicken or lamb kebabs, cut in narrow strips off a big hunk of meat roasted on a vertical spit (like the Turkish doner kebab) and served wrapped in flatbread with salad

tabbouleh finely chopped mixture of tomato, mint and cracked wheat

tahini paste made from sesame seeds

waraq aynab vine leaves stuffed with a mixture of rice and meat

zaatar a widely used seasoning made from a mixture of dried thyme (or oregano), salt and sesame seeds

zatoon olives

Glossary

abbeya black, full-length women's traditional robe

abra small boat used to ferry passengers across the Creek (see p.37 & p.116)

attar traditional perfume

bahar sea

barasti palm thatch used to construct traditional houses

bayt/bait house

burj tower

dar house

dhow generic term loosely used to describe all types of traditional wooden Arabian boat

dishdasha see *kandoura* below

Eid ul Fitr festival celebrating the end of Ramadan (see p.125)

falaj traditional irrigation technique used to water date plantations, with water drawn from deep underground and carried to its destination along tiny earthen canals

funduk hotel

ghutra men's headscarf, usually white or red-and-white check

haj pilgrimage to Mecca

hosn/hisn fort

iftar the breaking of the fast after dark during Ramadan

iqal the rope-like black cords used to keep the *ghutra* on the head (traditionally used to tie together the legs of camels to stop them running off)

jebel hill or mountain

kandoura the full-length traditional robe worn by Gulf Arabs (also known as *dishdashas*). A decorative tassel, known as the *farokha* (or *tarboush*), often hangs from the collar. A long robe, or *basht*, is sometimes worn over the *dishdasha* on formal occasions, denoting the authority of the wearer

Al Khaleej The Gulf (translated locally as the Arabian Gulf, never as the Persian Gulf)

khanjar traditional curved dagger, usually made of silver

Al Khor The Creek

majlis meeting/reception room in a traditional Arabian house; the place where local or family problems were discussed and decisions taken

mashrabiya projecting window protected by a carved wooden latticework screen – although the term is often loosely used to describe any kind of elaborately carved latticework screen, whether or not a window is also present

masjid mosque

mina port

nakheel palm tree

oud Arabian lute; also the name of a key ingredient in Arabian perfumes derived from agarwood

qasr palace or castle

qibla the direction of Mecca, usually indicated by a sign or sticker in most hotel rooms in the city (and in mosques by a recessed niche known as the mihrab)

Ramadan see p.124

shayla women's black headscarf, worn with an *abbeya*

wadi dry river bed or valley

PUBLISHING INFORMATION

This first edition published March 2014 by **Rough Guides Ltd**

80 Strand, London WC2R 0RL

11, Community Centre, Panchsheel Park, New Delhi 110017, India

Distributed by the Penguin Group

Penguin Books Ltd, 80 Strand, London WC2R 0RL

Penguin Group (USA) 345 Hudson Street, NY 10014, USA

Penguin Group (Australia) 250 Camberwell Road, Camberwell, Victoria 3124, Australia

Penguin Group (NZ) 67 Apollo Drive, Mairangi Bay, Auckland 1310, New Zealand

Penguin Group (South Africa) Block D, Rosebank Office Park, 181 Jan Smuts Avenue, Parktown North, Gauteng, South Africa 2193

Rough Guides is represented in Canada by

Tourmaline Editions Inc., 662 King Street West, Suite 304, Toronto, Ontario, M5V 1M7

Typeset in Minion and Din to an original design by Henry Iles and Dan May.

Printed and bound in China

© Rough Guides 2014

Maps © Rough Guides

136pp includes index

A catalogue record for this book is available from the British Library

ISBN 978-1-40932-234-4

MIX
Paper from responsible sources
FSC www.fsc.org   FSC™ C018179

ROUGH GUIDES CREDITS

Text editor: Edward Aves

Layout: Jessica Subramanian

Cartography: Katie Bennett

Picture editors: Mark Thomas, Tim Draper

Photographer: Tim Draper

Production: Linda Dare

Proofreader: Jan McCann

Cover design: Wilf Matos and Jessica Subramanian

THE AUTHOR

Gavin Thomas has worked for Rough Guides as a writer and editor since 1998; he is also the author of the *Rough Guide to Oman* and the *Rough Guide to Sri Lanka*, and co-author of the *Rough Guide to Rajasthan, Delhi & Agra*.

HELP US UPDATE

We've gone to a lot of effort to ensure that the first edition of the **Pocket Rough Guide Dubai** is accurate and up-to-date. However, things change – places get "discovered", opening hours are notoriously fickle, restaurants and rooms raise prices or lower standards. If you feel we've got it wrong or left something out, we'd like to know, and if you can remember the address, the price, the hours, the phone number, so much the better.

Please send your comments with the subject line "**Pocket Rough Guide Dubai Update**" to ⊜ mail@roughguides.com. We'll credit all contributions and send a copy of the next edition (or any other Rough Guide if you prefer) for the very best emails.

Find more travel information, connect with fellow travellers and book your trip on ⊛ roughguides.com

PHOTO CREDITS

All images © Rough Guides except the following:
(Key: t-top; c-centre; b-bottom; l-left; r-right)

Front cover Burj Khalifa © Superstock/Jose Fuste Raga/Prisma
Back cover Abra on the Creek © Rough Guides/Tim Draper
p.1 Getty Images/Jochen Tack
p.2 Getty Images/Jonathan Kitchen
p.4 Getty Images/Katarina Premfors
p.5 The Address Downtown Dubai Hotel/Nicolas Dumont
p.8 Getty Images/JD Dallet (c)
p.9 Alamy Images/iDubai (c)
p.15 Getty Images/Lars Ruecker (b)
p.16 Alamy Images/Travelstock44
p.18 Chris Cypert/Chris Cypert
p.19 Buddha Bar/Nicolas Dumont (t); courtesy of La Petite Maison (cl); courtesy of Table 9 by Nick and Scott/Mike Malate (cr); Indego by Vineet/Nicolas Dumont (b)

p.22 Courtesy of Jumeirah Zabeel Saray Hotel
p.23 Courtesy of Grosvenor House Hotel (t); Alamy Images/Peter Bowater (b)
p.24 Getty Images/Visions Of Our Land
p.25 Wild Wadi/Maurizio Rellini (t); Alamy Images/Peter Stroh (cr)
p.27 Courtesy of One&Only The Palm (t); Bar 44/Nicolas Dumont (c); One&Only Royal Mirage/Nicolas Dumont (b)
p.30 Getty Images/Xu Jian
p.73 Courtesy of Burj al Arab
p.78 Courtesy of Burj al Arab – Al Mahara
p.86 Eauzone/Antonie Robertson
p.95 Alamy Images/Phil Dunne
p.102 Courtesy of Burj Al Arab – Club Suite
p.112 Getty Images/Xu Jian

Index

Maps are marked in **bold**.